MAKAN

MAKAN

RECIPES FROM THE HEART OF SINGAPORE

ELIZABETH HAIGH

Photography by
Kris Kirkham

BLOOMSBURY ABSOLUTE
LONDON · OXFORD · NEW YORK · NEW DELHI · SYDNEY

introduction

In my family, aside from each other, food is everything. It's our family's legacy. We talk about food constantly, from what we are going to be having for dinner while eating breakfast, or what my mum will be making this week. It's almost like living in a chaotic restaurant, so I guess it was a natural progression that I ended up becoming a chef.

I put in the hours and quickly progressed through the ranks until I became head chef of several restaurants, one of which was Pidgin in Hackney in London, where we were awarded a Michelin star in 2016. I was only 27. Straight away this gave me the drive and energy to focus on my own projects and ideas leading towards what I had neglected – my heritage. So I wanted to open a *kopitiam*, or coffee shop (that also sells food).

In Singapore it's very common to greet each other with 'Are you hungry?' or 'Shall we go get some food?' rather than 'Hello, how are you?'. This is because we live by our stomachs and are very proud of it too. Singapore is a mecca for all sorts of cuisines. It's impossible to pinpoint where dishes have come from, so when people ask me what food is Singaporean, I simply reply: 'the delicious type'. Southeast Asian cuisine is a proud mix of migrants and influences from all across Asia, and from afar, which fuses together to create something even greater than the original.

In the UK I've found that a lot of people don't know where Singapore actually is, and if they do, it is usually because they've been in the airport on their way to a connecting flight to somewhere else. Although the airport is very impressive, it isn't the real Singapore, nor does it represent the Singapore that I love and appreciate. Singapore is not all about the glam – the butterfly gardens or designer shops. To me, the heart of Singapore is in its belly: the food.

Peranakan Chinese and Straits-born Chinese are the descendants of Chinese immigrants from the southern provinces who settled in Malaysia and Singapore. Intermarriage resulted in a distinctive culture of Straits-Peranakan whose language, clothing, art and cooking are celebrated to this day. The unique fusion food combines Chinese with influences from Malay, Indian, Thai, Indonesian, Dutch, Portuguese and, of course, English cuisine. It's simply the definition of island cuisine.

Peranakan men refer to themselves as 'Baba' (Uncle), while women are 'Nonya' (Auntie). It's no surprise the cuisine is called Nonya after the women: the matriarchal recipes are passed down from generation to generation and every woman is expected to master them. Indeed, a prospective bride has to prove to her potential mother-in-law that she can cook sufficiently well to ensure her son will be looked after properly following marriage. I'm lucky my in-laws are based in Australia, so I didn't get as much of a 'grilling' as my mother would have had.

These recipes are usually passed down orally, therefore you have to master them from memory. It's always a battle to get these secret family recipes, but I have long wanted to write them down properly, to log them and create a time-capsule of a cuisine that is so significant to many back home. I'm ashamed to say that, like many Singaporeans, I really never saw the importance of learning or mastering these dishes because my mum cooked them so well. The same applies in Singapore as you're always guaranteed good food from a hawker only a stone's throw away. So why would you put yourself through the hassle of buying ingredients, prepping and cooking?

My Singaporean family, the Yeos.

The best way to eat durian, on a floor covered in newspaper.
Left to right: Uncle Tony, Auntie Kim, my mother and me, aged 3.

Hawkers in Singapore are facing a problem. The hawker centres are home to the best food stalls in the world. These Aunties and Uncles, usually hunched-over leathery-skinned geriatrics, each specialise in one dish, and make and sell it until they can no longer hold the stall, then they retire. In addition to simply getting older, there's the stress of constantly rising rents and increasing food prices. Once gone their hawker knowledge, experience and passion is lost. They work incredibly hard so their children can get a good education and a 'proper job'. The younger generation don't want to do the graft for such low marginal gains. When I told Uncle at my local *kopitiam* (coffee shop) in Singapore that I had opened up my own *kopitiam* in London, he thought I was mad. 'But you have a degree *lah*? Why bother? Go work in an office!'

My father was temporarily stationed in Singapore when I was born, and we moved back to England when I was only a few months old. My sisters and I were brought up on predominantly Asian food because that's what my mother knew how to cook at the time. The cuisine in the early 1980s in the UK simply baffled her. Back home in Singapore she was the eldest of five and aged about 11 she was in charge of looking after and cooking for her family, while my grandparents worked. So, cooking for her was second nature and she loved to feed us all. When my parents married, she cooked my father a different meal every day for 2 years, without repeating anything – and I thought changing a menu every week at a restaurant was hard! Her way of showing and showering us with love is through her cooking, not only to feed a primal demand, but to put such care into it that it always makes us smile and feel better.

Growing up in England, my sisters and I were fascinated by all the types of food that we had access to. Mum studied for City and Guilds qualifications for making wedding cakes and incredibly impressive sugar work. I used to be very naughty and would secretly eat her sugar flowers, which had taken her weeks to make. My sister Jane, being the youngest, always somehow managed to cover herself in flour. Her nickname was and still is *chilli padi* (bird's eye chilli), meaning a pint-sized aggressive person. (Anyone who knows her knows this is true.) So, we were pretty much kept out of the kitchen. It was my mother's domain (I call it her organised chaos), and we would be scolded endlessly if we moved or touched anything without her knowing.

When my sisters and I went off to university we felt a huge displacement without our home-cooked food. That's when I started to take cooking seriously and my passion for it grew: it was my only connection to home. I felt frustrated that I had taken my mother's cooking for granted and refused to settle for beans on toast for dinner while I was studying (although I do have a soft spot for beans on toast). I constantly bombarded my mum with emails, messages and calls, asking for step-by-step instructions on how to make my favourite dishes that would comfort me when I was feeling overwhelmed with my university workload. I'm certain my sisters did the exact same thing. Most of the time I'd get a very brief response from my mum – for example, for her crispy roast pork recipe it was 'prick skin and roast it'.

However, if she did share her recipes with me, her instructions were rather difficult to follow and I faced many challenges along the way. It began with my having to translate hard-to-read handwritten notes, or convert measurements, and moved on to learning about the different *daun* (herbs) or *rempahs* (spice pastes). Technique aside, ingredients were hard to find, but thankfully I was just a bus ride away from Chinatown in Central London. So I adapted my larder and stock cupboard to include a different arrangement of spices and ingredients, which baffled some of my university flatmates. I believe my fermented tofu and cabbage still haunt them to this day. One incident stays with me: I left a jar of *belachan* (fermented shrimp paste) out and open. My flatmate's cat got into it and later left a incredibly smelly cat litter tray. We couldn't get rid of the stench from the flat for weeks!

The one question I get asked all the time is 'Where are you from?'. As a child this baffled me because I'd lived in England nearly all my life, so I would always answer, 'Where I was born or where I currently reside?' Back then, in the early 1990s, I could never understand why there was such a need to know where a person was from, and the usual 'You're not from around here' would always hurt just that little bit. But now, as an adult, I embrace my heritage and culture and am proud to stand out.

The more I learned and experimented with the food, the more I felt connected back to my heritage. I spent four hard years studying for a diploma in Classical Cookery while working as a chef in a restaurant full time – long days in school and then long evenings in the restaurant. Compared to my classical French cookery training, Nonya cooking feels very sensual, because it's a dash of this, a splash of that – very much from the heart and taste buds rather than following a written recipe. So you could say that this collection of recipes could be taken with a pinch of salt? Or sugar?

I needed to adapt and create recipes that replaced or included ingredients that I could find locally and seasonally. For example, it can be difficult to get hold of specific Chinese greens but they are easily replaced with what is fresh in the UK. My mother's recipes also contained a lot of *agak agak*, or 'guesstimation', because she never believed that there is an exact measurement for dishes – you must rely on personal taste and adjust according to how many you are cooking for and what ingredients you have available. The chillies in Europe are going to have a different taste and heat compared to chillies grown in Southeast Asian sunlight. And everyone has their own ability to handle chilli heat in their food. I've written these recipes according to what I prefer, and you should try to do the same, adapting them to your preference. If you like hot food, increase the dried or fresh chillies, or if you want more sour notes, add extra acidity with lime juice or tamarind. Be brave and experiment!

I quickly learnt the importance of: 1) a good blender, which will save you mountains of time and arm power, 2) the 'holy trinity' of Singaporean cooking – garlic, shallots and ginger – which is the basis of 3) *rempahs* (spice pastes). My mum was passionate about pounding the *rempah* in her huge mortar and pestle, but my blender is incredibly strong, and used correctly, by adding the ingredients in the right order, I've found it gives the same effect.

Although I ate this food growing up, and experimented with it as a university student, it wasn't until after I had been working as a chef for a number of years – and having trained as a chef in classic French cooking – that I really applied a trained chef mentality to the learning. After I got over the initial anxiety about really learning this cuisine, and breaking old habits and learning new ones, it became a walk in the park. Along this journey, I've learnt a lot about the Nonya culture and appreciate it even more now.

This project has been about collecting, adapting and understanding these recipes because I didn't want them to be lost. And I wanted to share them with you to enjoy. I had my first son Riley in 2017, and it's crucial to me that he and my husband, Steele, learn about our heritage. Food felt like a wonderful way to do this. Despite having the difficulties of feeding a toddler, Riley adores the rice dishes and I've adapted some of these recipes to make them baby-friendly. I just omit the salt, sugar and chilli and add them in later for myself. Some of these recipes are a fusion of traditional Nonya cooking and my experience as a chef in London, or what I love to cook at home with my family.

Every year we celebrate traditions, such as Chinese New Year, with certain dishes. Similarly, if anyone is ill or under the weather, we cook particular dishes to help us feel better. A lot of Chinese cuisine, including Nonya cuisine, is considered to have medicinal purposes, and is not just for eating pleasure.

This book will give you an insight into our family's repertoire of meals, developed over the years and married with what's available seasonally. Cuisine cannot exist without the fair and free movement of ingredients, ideas and people. Deliciousness is an undeniable benefit of migration and that's exactly what my family has achieved. When people move and mix together, food just gets better. I'm proud that this collection of recipes is inauthentic, but they have the same satisfying effect as eating back home. They are authentic to me because they are my history, my journey and the reflection of my family as it has grown and developed over the years.

The book has been divided into chapters that I would construct a meal from. Typically, a Chinese-Singaporean meal consists of a protein dish (a fish or meat main course), a rice dish, a soup and a vegetable side (or main). I've also added a chapter of dishes that require a little more time and attention, usually for a celebration or occasion meal.

Being a chef, I find that good-quality produce and using the best ingredients will improve any dish without you needing to try hard. So source from the right shops. You can find an Asian-produce supermarket in most neighbourhoods, and many stock cupboard ingredients can be sourced online. If you struggle to find the right fresh ingredients, such as Chinese *kai lan* or *choi sum* greens, which are sometimes imported from abroad, remember that they can be replaced with something easily found here such as spinach, chard or kale.

It's been an exciting journey, but essentially this is a home cookbook, to be used and bruised in the kitchen – recipes for you to master and to pass down the generations to enjoy.

the traditional kitchen

These days in Singapore it's becoming more common for new-builds to be constructed without a kitchen, to save space, because there is little demand for a place to cook. I remember distinctly our old kitchen in Bukit Batok before we moved to another area in Singapore. It was a hot, sticky room with a marble floor that was always cool to the touch. My mother and grandmother would cover the floor with newspaper and the family would sit down to break open and tuck into durians, or they'd lay a thick chopping board on the cool floor and chop through a cooked chicken (instead of carving it). The pantry on the cooler side of the house, away from the windows, was where things like rice and sauces were kept.

My mother always had a chopping board next to the sink, even sometimes balanced over it, where she would prepare ingredients like fish, meat or chicken, discarding the rubbish or trimmings into the sink. Like her grandmother, my mum kept her most frequently used condiments and ingredients within easy reach of where she cooked. That often meant a plastic tray full of little jars of oils, crispy-fried shallots or garlic, crushed garlic, salt and sugar. There was also usually an old metal pot for recycled or discarded frying oil.

On the shelf underneath the stove, my mother had bottles of soy sauce, cooking wine, vinegars, you name it – everything you could think of. The pantry was the dry store area with a big plastic container of rice, which we bought in 20kg bags because it was cheaper that way. We ate rice nearly every day, and I will never tire of it. Next to the rice was a three-tiered plastic trolley, full of garlic, ginger, shallots and dried chillies. In the fridge, well, let's just say everything but the kitchen sink would be in there: a drawer full of fresh chillies, pandan leaves, *belachan* (in a sealed container!), dried shrimps, kaffir lime leaves, coriander leaves and more.

In my own kitchen, I prefer to buy fresh ingredients on the day, but only if I can source the best on that day. I think that ingredients like coriander don't keep well, but here's a chef's trick to extend shelf life: wash it well, drain it and spin it in a salad spinner, then wrap a damp J-cloth round it and keep in the fridge.

ingredients

dry spices

My mother would sometimes have spices in her cupboard that would be older than me!

The shelf life of spices can range from 6 months to 2 years, but they will lose their aroma over time. So I tend to replace my spices after 6 months. And I never buy too much at a time. I usually go to a loose spice shop where you can get the quantity you want, rather than buying those tiny, and expensive, jars of spice in the supermarket. The best way to store spices is in airtight containers (my mother used to be a Tupperware representative so we had plenty of plastic containers in all shapes and sizes). Generally whole spices retain their flavour and aroma better than ground spices, so I prefer to buy them whole and grind as needed. Spice grinders are so cheap, and a high-speed blender will also do the job.

fresh herbs and vegetables

These ingredients are the trickiest aspect of cooking Nonya cuisine here in the UK, because the quality of fresh herbs and vegetables really depends on when they were imported and how they were kept. Ingredients such as beansprouts or coriander can wilt and discolour after just one day, so I always try to buy these fresh on the day of use. Most supermarkets now stock ingredients such as lemongrass, mooli or white radish, ginger, beansprouts and spring onions. I usually head to an oriental store to shop for galangal and more specialist items like torch ginger and pandan leaves. Chinese greens such as *kai lan*, *kangkong* (water spinach) and *choi san* are much harder to find. However, you can normally find *pak choi* and *choi sum* in supermarkets these days, although at a much higher price than from an Asian supermarket.

dried ingredients

Many dried ingredients, such as those used in Chap Chai (see page 48) or Bak Kut Teh (page 163), can be purchased from Chinese medicine shops. They are often better quality than the packaged ones you find in the dry goods section of oriental stores. When in doubt, just show a picture and ask.

noodles

Dried noodles are sold in various sized packages but within the packets the noodles are normally bundled up in portion sizes. So if a recipe refers to a bundle, it will mean this. Dried noodles need to be rehydrated before use, so put them into a bowl and pour over hot water to cover. Rehydrating time will depend on the size of the noodle – dried vermicelli (such as *bee hoon, mee sua* and glass / beanthread), for example, are very quick: you'd want to drain them after a minute or two, then run under cold water to stop them from sticking together in a clump.

To untangle some fresh noodles, such as flat rice noodles (*kway teow*), it is best to microwave them in 10-second blasts until they can be pulled apart. Alternatively, blanch with warm water, then rinse with cold (otherwise the noodles will just disintegrate), or just rinse in lukewarm water to help separate them, then drain well.

crispy shallots

I use crispy shallots on nearly every soup dish, because I love the crunchy texture they add, as well as that extra kick of saltiness and onion flavour that complements stocks so well. It's simple to make your own crispy shallots and you then also have the oil for dressings (see the recipe for Shallot Oil / Crispy Shallots on page 268). I run out of crispy shallots often, as well as time to make them, so I don't see any shame in buying crisp-fried onions or garlic slices in large jars. They keep well in a dark, cool cupboard.

other ingredients

I prefer to use bottled sauces and ingredients with few additives and preservatives. This is particularly important for me when I cook for Riley. The following list includes the items I always have in my cupboards, as well as buying tips for fresh poultry and fish.

caster sugar   I always use caster sugar in my dishes because its fine texture means it dissolves faster than granulated.

chicken   I recommend you buy free-range, organic chicken from a butcher that you know and trust. You can tell a chicken is good if the skin isn't broken and it has a bright appearance.

cornflour   This is always on hand to make a quick slurry to thicken sauces.

fish   I recommend that you always buy the best-quality sustainable fish, from a trusted source such as a good fishmonger, and never buy on a Sunday, Monday or Tuesday as these are the days the fishermen aren't out at sea. In this book I mostly use sea bass, salmon, sea bream and mackerel.

fish sauce   Commonly used to add extra saltiness and fishy flavour. Some cheaper brands tend to be way too salty for my liking. My favourite brands are Squid or Mega Chef. Fish sauce has a pretty funky smell, so don't spill it in your kitchen.

monosodium glutamate (MSG)   Despite its bad reputation, this is an essential ingredient to Chinese cooking. My family would have a large pot next to their stove, which they would add into cooking, just like salt. MSG adds more umami flavour, and it is found naturally in a lot of ingredients such as anchovies, tomatoes or mushrooms.

oils   We usually use groundnut oil for cooking and deep-frying, but canola oil and vegetable oil, which are slightly lower in saturated fat, can also be used. My mum uses rice bran oil. For the recipes in this book, any unflavoured oil with a high burning temperature, such as vegetable, rapeseed or sunflower oil, will work when the recipe calls for 'cooking oil'.

pepper   Unless specified, ground white pepper is used for seasoning in all recipes. White pepper is actually hotter than black pepper and is produced from soaking black peppercorns in water until the outer black skin disintegrates, thus exposing the more intense core of the peppercorn. Pepper is thought to aid digestion.

rice wine & shaoxing (*hua diao*)	If you ever wondered why your home-made Chinese food doesn't taste like what you'd get at a restaurant, shaoxing wine may be the key missing element! Most rice wines have a lighter flavour than Chinese shaoxing wine, which then adds a richer flavour to dishes. You can also use Japanese sake as a substitute if you cannot find shaoxing wine, and if you truly can't locate a bottle of rice wine, substitute a dry cooking sherry.
salt	My mum uses table salt but I much prefer to use Cornish Sea Salt Co flakes or crystals, unless the recipe calls for a lot of salt such as when making brines.
soy sauce	**Chinese dark soy sauce:** This is usually made with the addition of molasses or caramel for a dark rich colour and flavour. Mushroom-flavoured superior dark soy sauce will add a rich, aniseedy, meaty flavour to dishes like stir-fries and soups. **Light soy sauce:** Our preferred brands are Pearl River Bridge or Amoy. **Sweet soy sauce:** Also known as *kecap manis*, this is perfect served alongside our Hainanese Chicken Rice (see page 196). My son loves the Healthy Boy brand.
toasted sesame oil	We use this as a seasoning. The pure sesame oil by Chee Seng is the best. Don't use it for frying as it has a low burning point so it will smoke and burn easily, giving a horrible taste.
vinegar	Chinese vinegars are made mainly from fermented rice of various types, although other grains are also used. **Red rice vinegar:** This is red-brown in colour and tart yet mild. It is used mainly as a finishing touch for seafood soups. **White rice vinegar:** This is less acidic than Western white wine vinegar, closer to cider vinegar but without the fruity undertones. **Black rice vinegar (Chinkiang Vinegar):** This has a malty, complex taste that is perfect for dressings and as a dipping sauce for dumplings. You could substitute balsamic vinegar for the latter (as long as it isn't too sweet and syrupy), but if you are going to the effort of making the recipe, find black vinegar in stores.

techniques

blending the *rempah*

As mentioned before, mastering the *rempah* (spice paste) will take half the work out of a recipe. It's important when pounding the ingredients in a mortar and pestle, or using a food processor or blender, that you add the ingredients in a certain order. This will ensure a much finer paste.

The harder and drier ingredients, such as candlenuts and spice seeds, are ground first followed by the galangal, turmeric and lemongrass in that order. Next the shallots, garlic and fresh chillies are blended in. Soaked dried chillies are then added. I use some of the warm chilli-soaking water to help blend the paste together if required. *Belachan* (fermented shrimp paste), with its pasty putty-like texture, is mixed in last. It's incredibly salty so make sure it is well crumbled and blended in, and take care not to add too much. You can always add more salt at the end.

frying the *rempah*

I learnt this technique the hard way. Initially I thought faster and higher heat would achieve a quicker result, but it just meant I had to stir the *rempah* a lot. I got hot *rempah* splashed into my eye and swore I couldn't see properly for an hour. You just can't speed this part up. Heat the oil on a controlled medium heat in a heavy-based pan, like a Le Creuset, until it starts to glisten and sizzle. Add the *rempah* and stir constantly so it doesn't scorch or burn on the bottom of the pan. After all the effort you went to in blending the *rempah*, you don't want to have it catch on the base of the pan, which would give a burnt aftertaste to the dish. Also you'd have some serious washing-up to do.

If the oil starts to smoke, turn the heat right down, or even take the pan off the heat. As the paste cooks, it will release an intense aroma and deepen in colour. When the *keluar minyah* ('oil arises'), or seeps out of the paste, the oil will have turned a rich red colour from the chillies or yellow from the turmeric and galangal, which signifies the *rempah* is ready.

agak agak By tradition, Nonya Aunties engaged all their senses when they cooked. It was really important to gauge the smells and colour of the gravy; feel the warmth of the charcoal or wok heat; listen to the sizzle of the *rempah*; and – the best bit – taste constantly. The Aunties cooked by *agak agak*, or 'guesstimation'. This meant that passed-down recipes were totally inexact and is why I've struggled so much with this project.

The only person who can really know what you like and prefer is yourself. If you want to have a sweeter dish, you'll add more sugar. For more sour add more tamarind or lime. The cook has complete control of how she (or he) wants the dish to be. These recipes are just guidelines to start you off.

The quality and availability of ingredients have changed dramatically over the years since I was little, in the 1980s when we emigrated to the UK. So a lot of my mum's recipes don't include ingredients that I would now use. This, though, was just the fun of adapting and re-working these recipes, and why I describe them as inauthentic.

I tend not to season too early because flavours develop or deepen as the cooking process continues. This particularly applies to anything containing prawns, stocks, *belachan* and, especially, fermented soya-bean paste (*taucheo*). So in making these recipes, use your senses, and feel free to *agak* how much of something to add – more or less, according to your own taste.

nonya
secrets

The recipes in this chapter are the heart of this book. I had to drag them out of my mother and get them from her head down on to paper. It was probably the hardest chapter to write because the recipes were so far out of my usual comfort zone. Mum would always just whip them up without much hassle but whenever I tried to learn, I found there were so many secret tips and techniques that weren't part of my catering knowledge or experience as a chef.

I find the best way to approach the recipes is to read them carefully and to prepare as much as you can before you start cooking. Usually this means to prepare the vegetables, or the protein part of a dish, and blend a *rempah* (spice paste). Then you can put everything together. Once you master these recipes, the dishes in the rest of the book will be a breeze.

Nonya food is tangy, aromatic, spicy and herbal. Nonya curry dishes are more on the fragrant side than just powerful spice heat. I adore this cuisine because it really plays on all your senses and your tongue with multiple sweet and sour notes. Key ingredients for Nonya and Peranakan cuisine are coconut milk, lemongrass, tamarind, galangal and turmeric.

These recipes aren't quick to make – the longer you marinate the meat, or pound the *rempah* ingredients together carefully, the better the result you'll get. It's said that the Aunties – and prospective mothers-in-law – could always tell the calibre of a chef (or woman) just by the sound of the pestle hitting the mortar when pounding the ingredients. Sorry Mum, a blender works just as well for me, although I pulse the ingredients bit by bit and then bring it all together, to mimic the bruising you'd obtain from a pestle and mortar.

"Mee Soto"
Spiced Chicken Noodle Soup

I take after my mother so I always make enough chicken stock to make multiple meals, enough to feed an army. This recipe is easy to put together and really combines the essence of Nonya cuisine with its aromatic, spicy and herbal notes.

SERVES 4–6

1 whole chicken, about 1.5kg
2 tablespoons cooking oil
200g dried glass vermicelli
    (beanthread vermicelli), soaked
    in hot water to rehydrate and
    drained
200g beansprouts, topped and
    tailed, blanched for 30 seconds
a bunch of spring onions (green
    part), finely chopped
a bunch of coriander, leaves picked
5 tablespoons Crispy Shallots
    (see page 268)
lime quarters
salt

For the rempah
10 candlenuts or macadamia nuts
4 tablespoons coriander seeds
1 tablespoon white peppercorns
1 tablespoon cumin seeds
a 2.5cm piece of fresh galangal,
    peeled and julienned
a 2.5cm piece of fresh turmeric,
    peeled and julienned, or
    2 teaspoons ground turmeric
a 5cm piece of root ginger, peeled
    and julienned
2 stalks of lemongrass (bottom
    third), smashed and finely sliced
20 small shallots, peeled and
    quartered
5 garlic cloves, peeled

Put the chicken in a large saucepan and cover with cold water. Bring to the boil, then turn down the heat and simmer the chicken for about 1 hour or until tender and cooked through. Transfer the chicken to a platter. Reserve the stock.

Once cool enough to touch, remove the meat from the carcass and shred with the skin.

To make the *rempah*, grind the ingredients together in a blender (adding them in the order listed) to make a paste. Add a little water if necessary.

Heat the oil in a large saucepan and stir-fry the *rempah* over a low heat until fragrant, being very careful not to burn it. Add the reserved chicken stock and bring to the boil. Season with salt.

To serve, divide the vermicelli among the bowls and add the blanched beansprouts and shredded chicken. Ladle enough soup into the bowls to cover the noodles. Garnish with spring onions, coriander and crispy shallots. Add a squeeze of lime juice if liked.

"Sayur Lodeh"
Coconut Vegetable Curry

This is a dish of vegetables simmered in a coconut milk curry, popular in Indonesia and Malaysia. We love it on the side with our Nasi Lemak (see page 193). You can adjust the heat and spice of the curry to your own taste. Omit the prawns, dried shrimp and *belachan* if you want to make this a vegetarian or vegan dish, but add an extra teaspoon of salt to balance the flavours.

SERVES 4

½ white cabbage
150g long beans or French beans
4 tablespoons cooking oil
2 thick slices of fresh galangal, peeled
60g dried shrimps, soaked, drained and finely chopped
800ml water
a 400ml can coconut milk, coconut cream skimmed off the top and reserved
1 carrot, peeled and cut diagonally into bite-sized pieces
4 tofu puffs, about 80g in total, each cut in half
200g compressed rice cakes, cut into 2.5cm pieces (optional)
115g peeled raw prawns (optional)
1 teaspoon salt

For the rempah
5 shallots, peeled and roughly chopped
2 garlic cloves, peeled
6 dried red chillies (or 1 teaspoon chilli powder)
1 teaspoon ground turmeric
1 teaspoon ground coriander
1 teaspoon *belachan* (fermented shrimp paste) (optional)

Cut the cabbage leaves and long beans into bite-sized pieces.

Grind all the *rempah* ingredients together in a blender to make a paste. Heat the oil in a large saucepan and fry the *rempah* until fragrant. Keep it moving or it will catch at the bottom. Add the galangal slices and dried shrimps and continue to stir-fry for a few minutes.

Pour in the water and thin coconut milk, and bring to the boil. Add the carrot, beans and tofu puffs and stir well. Simmer for about 10 minutes or until the vegetables are tender. Add the cabbage and rice cake, if using, and cook for a further 2 minutes or until soft. If using the prawns, add them just at the end, cooking for 2–3 minutes or until they change colour. Add the salt and check the seasoning. Remove the thick galangal slices if preferred.

Finish off by stirring in the reserved coconut cream. Serve hot.

Literally translating as mix-mix, this is a mixed salad of blanched, boiled or steamed vegetables along with *lontong* (compressed rice cakes) that's mixed around in a rich sweet and sour peanut sauce.

First prepare the peanut sauce. Drain the soaked chillies, then grind with the shallots, garlic and *belachan* in a blender to make a fine paste, using some of the leftover chilli water if necessary.

Heat the oil in a wok over a low heat to about 160°C, then fry the peanuts for 4–5 minutes or until golden, stirring constantly. Using a slotted spoon, carefully lift the peanuts out of the oil and drain on kitchen paper. Crush the peanuts in a food processor until chunky or smooth, depending on your preference.

Pour off most of the oil from the wok (reserve some for frying the tofu later). Add the chilli paste to the wok and fry until fragrant.

Add 375ml of the tamarind juice, followed by the sugars and salt. Stir until they all dissolve. Add the rice wine vinegar and crushed peanuts and bring to the boil. Lower the heat and simmer until the sauce has a slightly thicker consistency. Add the remaining tamarind juice and the coconut milk. If the sauce is too thick for your liking, add more coconut milk.

Bring a pot of salted water to the boil. First blanch the cabbage for about 1 minute; remove with a spider or slotted spoon, then blanch the green beans for 1 minute and remove. Finally blanch the beansprouts for about 30 seconds. You want all the vegetables to have a little bite so don't overcook. After each vegetable is drained, refresh it in iced water to stop the cooking process. Drain and pat dry well.

Heat some of the peanut oil in a frying pan and shallow-fry the tofu until a light golden brown all over. Rest on a plate lined with kitchen paper to absorb the excess oil.

To serve, arrange a bit of each vegetable on 4 large plates with the eggs, tofu and rice cakes. Add a bowl of peanut sauce and prawn crackers on the side. Let the guests toss their own gado gado before eating.

SERVES 4

For the peanut sauce
45g dried red chillies, soaked in hot water for 30 minutes
70g banana shallots, diced
30g garlic, peeled
2 teaspoons *belachan* (fermented shrimp paste)
250ml cooking oil
340g shelled peeled peanuts, blanched
1 quantity Tamarind Juice (see page 269)
60g caster sugar
30g palm sugar, shaved or crumbled
40g soft brown or demerara sugar
10g salt
2 tablespoons rice wine vinegar
about 75ml canned coconut milk

For the salad
½ head white cabbage, leaves cut into 2.5cm squares
150g green beans, trimmed and cut into 5cm pieces
150g beansprouts, topped and tailed
150g firm tofu, cut into 4 pieces
½ head lettuce, leaves cut into 2.5cm squares
1 cucumber, deseeded and cut into bite-sized pieces
4 hard-boiled eggs, peeled and quartered
300g compressed rice cakes, cut into 2.5cm pieces (optional)
prawn crackers

Malay Hot and Sour Noodles

My mum told me this about Mee Siam: 'This is a staple breakfast dish in our family. The Singaporean taste is for the wet saucy version of the dish. I love to squeeze the juice from small fresh limes into the soup at the end and slurp it up. The perfect balance of the light gravy should be spicy and tangy with a tinge of sweetness.'

The garnish can be prepared in advance. Shallow-fry the tofu until brown on all sides, then drain and cut into 1cm cubes. Boil the prawns until just cooked, then peel and cut in half lengthways.

Grind together the *rempah* ingredients in a blender (adding them in the order listed) to make a fine paste.

Soak the vermicelli in hot water for 10 minutes to soften, then drain well in a colander. Spread flat on a baking tray lined with baking parchment and set aside.

Heat the oil in a wok over a high heat. When the oil starts to sizzle, turn the heat down and add the *rempah*. Stir-fry until fragrant and a richly coloured red oil bubbles through, around 10 minutes.

To make the coconut spice stock, mix the fermented soya-bean paste, tamarind juice and thin coconut milk in a saucepan. Bring to the boil, then turn down to a simmer. If the stock is too salty, add sugar to taste, and add a touch more water if too thick. Stir well. Set aside.

Add the sliced red onions and beansprouts to the wok and stir-fry for a minute. Push the onions and beansprouts to one side of the wok and add the soaked vermicelli. Stir really well to coat them with the spice paste and mix with the onions and beansprouts, taking care not to break up the noodles. Cook on a simmer for 3 minutes, adding a little of the coconut spice stock to prevent sticking, and taking care not to overcook or the noodles will go mushy.

To serve, dish up the vermicelli and top with the fried tofu and prawns. Spoon the coconut spice stock over. Squeeze plenty of lime juice over and top with the chopped chives and hard-boiled eggs.

SERVES 4

500g dried rice vermicelli
   (*bee hoon*)
120ml cooking oil
150g fermented soya-bean paste
625ml Tamarind Juice (see
   page 269)
1 litre thin coconut milk (made by
   diluting a 425ml can of coconut
   milk with water)
2–6 tablespoons caster sugar
2 red onions, sliced
350g beansprouts, topped
   and tailed

For the rempah
6 candlenuts or macadamia nuts
20 small shallots, diced
4 garlic cloves, peeled
20 dried large, red chillies
5 tablespoons dried shrimps,
   soaked in hot water for 10
   minutes and patted dry
60g *belachan* (fermented shrimp
   paste), cut into small cubes

To garnish
cooking oil
4 pieces of firm tofu, about 250g
   in total
450g medium raw prawns
4 limes, halved
a bunch of Chinese chives,
   chopped into 2–3cm pieces
10 hard-boiled eggs, peeled
   and halved

Sardine Curry

This is a firm family favourite and a go-to when a warming, quick meal is required. This recipe exemplifies the Nonya *agak agak* principle – the ingredients you use and how hot you want the dish to be are entirely a matter of personal taste and what is available. Personally, our family likes it medium hot with lots of vegetables, especially aubergine (we tend to use a whole one), okra and Turkish green peppers, which are like big green chillies but long, succulent and mild.

SERVES 4

1 red onion, roughly chopped
4 garlic cloves, crushed
a 2–3cm piece of root ginger, peeled and cut into thick slices
3 tablespoons cooking oil
1 lemongrass stalk, trimmed and hard outer leaves removed
½ teaspoon Panch Phoron (see page 268)
1 tablespoon Nonya Fish Curry Powder (see page 267)
a 400ml can coconut milk, coconut cream skimmed off the top and reserved
½ aubergine, diced into 2cm pieces
4 fresh Turkish green peppers, cored and sliced into 5cm pieces
1 quantity Tamarind Juice (see page 269)
250g okra, topped and tailed, sliced diagonally into 3cm pieces
5 curry leaves
2 medium-sized tomatoes, quartered
½ teaspoon hot chilli powder, or to taste
2 x 400g cans sardines or pilchards (either in brine or tomato sauce), drained

Grind the red onion, garlic and ginger together in a blender, adding 1 tablespoon water to help form a paste. Heat the oil in a heavy-bottomed pot over a medium heat and gently fry the onion paste to brown it lightly.

Cut the lemongrass on a diagonal into 3cm pieces. Crush the pieces slightly with the back of a knife, then add to the pot and stir. Add the panch phoron and Nonya fish curry powder and stir well, then stir in 2 tablespoons of the thin coconut milk.

Add the aubergine pieces and stir well to ensure they are covered with the curry mix. Cook for 2 minutes. Add the Turkish green peppers with another 2 tablespoons of coconut milk. Simmer for about 10 minutes, stirring constantly to ensure that the curry mix is not sticking to the pan.

Pour in the tamarind juice and stir well, then add 100ml of the coconut milk together with the okra, curry leaves and tomatoes. Continue to simmer for about 5 minutes or until the aubergine is soft.

Stir in the chilli powder, the remaining coconut milk, the coconut cream and the sardines or pilchards. Bring to the boil, then simmer, stirring occasionally, for 5 minutes or until the fish is warmed through. Be careful not to break up the fish when you stir.

Check the seasoning and serve with freshly steamed rice.

Nonya-spiced Fish Pâté

Otak translates as 'brains' but don't let that put you off this recipe. The title simply refers to the soft, smooth, rich texture of the delicious fish mix.

Pour boiling water over the banana leaves to soften them, then wipe dry. With a pair of kitchen scissors, trim off the hard veins along the edges of the leaves. Cut half of the leaves into 25cm squares (you need 12). Cut the remaining leaves into small 8cm squares (you need 24).

Cut the fish into small pieces, then finely chop or blend into a paste.

Combine the coconut milk, egg, sugar, salt and cornflour in a bowl. Stir well to remove any lumps and set aside.

Pound or grind the coriander seeds, then sieve to achieve a fine powder. Tip into a blender and grind to a paste with the rest of the *rempah* aromatics, adding them in the order listed. Add to the coconut milk and egg mixture. Blend all together well, blending in batches if necessary.

Add the *rempah* mixture to the fish paste and mix well together.

Preheat the grill.

Lay one of the larger squares of banana leaf on the work surface. Place a smaller square of leaf in the middle of the large leaf and spread with 4 tablespoons of the fish paste. Cover the paste with another small square of banana leaf. Fold 2 opposite ends of the large base leaf over to close the parcel. Fold in the other 2 ends and fasten with 2 sharp toothpicks. Repeat until all the fish paste is used up.

Arrange the parcels on a baking tray and grill for about 15 minutes, turning the parcels over occasionally to cook all sides evenly. Serve the pâté in the parcels.

SERVES 12 GENEROUSLY

250g fresh banana leaves (or 450g frozen banana leaves, thawed – you need extra as they tend to tear more easily)
800g hake fillet, or a mix of mackerel and red snapper fillet, skinned and pinboned
230ml canned coconut milk
1 egg
1 tablespoon caster sugar
½ teaspoon salt
1 tablespoon cornflour

For the rempah
2 teaspoons coriander seeds
170g fresh galangal, peeled and julienned
30g fresh turmeric, peeled and julienned, or 2 teaspoons ground turmeric
85g lemongrass stalks (bottom third only), thinly sliced
110g banana shallots, diced
5 fresh, medium-hot, red Dutch chillies, roughly chopped
15 dried red chillies, soaked in hot water for approx. 15 minutes to soften, drained
30g *belachan* (fermented shrimp paste)

"Asam Ikan Pedas" Fish Curry

This is a classic Nonya dish, traditionally made with fish steaks. It has lots of gravy with hot and sour notes, so you need a fish that can stand up to this. In Singapore we would ask our local wet market man to cut a couple of steaks from a large Spanish mackerel, but there is an array of other amazing fish that you could use. It doesn't matter whether it's a white or oily fish, as long as it can hold its shape. For white fish, go for hake (not cod as it is too flaky) or use whole sea bream, slashed twice on each side to allow the juices to penetrate. Whole mackerel (UK sized) or salmon steaks work well too.

Torch ginger flower is a common ingredient in Nonya cuisine because it gives dishes a distinctive sour flavour. The leaf can be used in the same way as turmeric leaf. The fruit is also edible. Inside the individual pods that make up the fruit are pulp-coated seeds – like passion fruit pulp – which explode in the mouth. It's very difficult to find torch ginger in the UK, so I recommend replacing it with laksa leaves.

SERVES 4

4 tablespoons cooking oil
3 aubergines, cut into 2cm chunks
5 sprigs of laksa leaves (or torch
  ginger flower buds)
4 kaffir lime leaves
1 quantity Tamarind Juice
  (see page 269)
8 okra, cut into bite-sized pieces
1 medium-sized tomato, cut into
  bite-sized pieces
caster sugar, to taste
a 1.2–1.5kg sea bream or mackerel
salt

For the rempah
2 candlenuts or macadamia nuts
a 3cm piece of fresh galangal,
  peeled
2 lemongrass stalks, tough outer
  leaves removed and stalks
  roughly chopped
4 banana shallots, peeled and
  roughly chopped
2 garlic cloves, peeled
20 dried, medium-hot red chillies
10g *belachan* (fermented
  shrimp paste)

Grind all the *rempah* ingredients together in a blender (adding them in the order listed) to make a paste. If the paste becomes too thick, add a little water. Set aside.

Heat the oil in a wok over a medium heat then quickly fry the aubergine until golden brown all over. Remove the aubergine pieces with a slotted spoon and set aside on a plate covered in kitchen paper.

Keeping the pan on the heat, next sauté the *rempah* in the oil, stirring constantly, until a richly coloured oil starts to seep from it – about 10 minutes. Add the laksa and lime leaves, and continue to sauté for about 30 seconds or until fragrant.

Add the tamarind juice and bring to the boil. Add the fried aubergines, okra and tomato. Add sugar and salt to taste.

Lay the fish in the sauce and simmer for 10 minutes or until the fish is cooked.

Remove the laksa stalks, pull off the leaves and tear the leaves roughly into pieces. Sprinkle on to the gravy. Serve with steamed white rice.

Chicken and Potato Curry

Like most Nonya dishes, this simple Peranakan dish is about fragrance and gutsy depth rather than a spice-heavy curry. I like to add a touch of my own curry powder and to have a slightly thick gravy, but this is all down to preference. If you want the curry to be slightly looser and lighter, don't reduce or add too much coconut cream/milk. I prefer to use chicken thighs or drumsticks on the bone, but you could use a whole jointed chicken instead.

Grind all the *rempah* ingredients together in a blender (adding them in the order listed) to make a fine paste. Add a little water if needed to get the right consistency. Lightly dust some extra curry powder over the chicken pieces in a bowl.

Heat the oil in a wok or large saucepan on a medium heat and fry the *rempah*, stirring constantly to prevent it from burning, for about 5 minutes or until very fragrant and a richly coloured oil is seeping out.

Add the chicken, cassia bark and potatoes and stir well to coat everything with the spice paste. Add the thinner coconut milk from the can to the wok together with 400ml water or chicken stock. Bring to the boil, stirring really well to make sure the *rempah* isn't stuck to the bottom of the pan. There should be enough liquid to cover the chicken and potatoes. Add the reserved lemongrass ends and the curry leaf, if using. Leave to simmer, uncovered, for at least 30 minutes or until the chicken is cooked through.

Add the coconut cream and simmer for a further 15 minutes or until the chicken is falling off the bone and you've reached your desired consistency of gravy. Add the salt and MSG, if using. Garnish with coriander and chilli and serve with freshly steamed rice on the side.

SERVES 4–6

6 free-range chicken legs, separated into thighs and drumsticks (skin on)
about 2 tablespoons cooking oil
a piece of cassia bark (optional)
3 medium potatoes (such as Maris Piper), peeled and quartered
a 400ml can coconut milk, coconut cream skimmed off the top and reserved
400ml water or Chicken Stock (see page 279)
3 pieces of curry leaf (optional)
½ teaspoon sea salt
½ teaspoon MSG (optional)

For the rempah
a 2.5cm piece of root ginger, peeled and roughly sliced
2 lemongrass stalks, smashed and dry ends cut off (keep these)
5 banana shallots, chopped
6 garlic cloves, peeled
4 fresh, medium-hot, red Dutch chillies, roughly chopped
1 tablespoon ground coriander
1 tablespoon ground cumin
1 teaspoon ground turmeric
1 tablespoon Curry Powder (see page 267), plus a little extra

To garnish
½ bunch of coriander, leaves picked
fresh red chilli, deseeded and finely sliced (optional)

"Nonya Chap Chai"

Full of vegetables and flavour. You can adjust the vegetables you add to this according to what is in season. I like to add a small handful of black moss to this dish for extra texture.

SERVES 4

100g dried glass vermicelli
  (beanthread vermicelli)
5 pieces of dried shiitake
  mushrooms
25g dried black fungus mushrooms
20g dried lily buds
4 tablespoons cooking oil
2 slices root ginger, peeled
3 garlic cloves, finely chopped
a 20g piece of fermented
  soya-bean curd
1 small white cabbage, leaves cut
  into 3cm pieces
1 carrot, peeled and thinly sliced
8 small tofu puffs, about 160g
  in total
50g black moss (optional)
a pinch of caster sugar, or to taste
salt

Break the vermicelli in half and leave to soak in cold water until soft.

Soak the shiitake, black fungus and lily buds in another bowl of cold water until soft, then drain and cut into quarters or smaller pieces.

Heat a frying pan and add the cooking oil. Add the ginger slices followed by the garlic. Stir-fry for about 1 minute, then very carefully add the soya-bean curd with a tablespoon of water and stir for another minute.

Add the shiitake, black fungus, lily buds, cabbage and carrot and stir-fry for another minute. Add the tofu puffs and black moss, if using, with 2 tablespoons of water, stir and cover the pan. Cook on a lower heat for 5 minutes.

Drain the vermicelli and add to the vegetable mix. Stir gently together. Continue to cook on a low heat for a further 3 minutes. Season with the sugar and a little salt.

Different regions have their own unique take on this soup. This is my mum's version and is one of my dad's favourites. It is best served with rice as a hearty meal, with some mixed vegetable pickles alongside (see pages 274–275). I recommend making the stock the day before to get the maximum flavour and also spread the workload! If mutton is not available you can use lamb.

Put the mutton in a large pot. Fill the pot with enough water to cover the chunks of meat and bring to the boil. Boil for about 5 minutes, then discard the water. Rinse the chunks and clean the pot.

Return the chunks of meat to the clean pot and add the carrots, celery, lemongrass, onion and all the spice mix ingredients (you can put the spices in a small muslin bag if you prefer). Fill with fresh water to cover the meat and other ingredients. Bring to the boil, then lower the heat and simmer for 2½ hours or until the meat is tender and falling off the bone.

Remove the chunks of meat from the pot (discard the bones) and reserve. Allow the stock to cool, then discard all the vegetables and herbs. Chill the stock overnight so that the layer of fat that sets on the surface can be scooped off.

The next day, prepare the *rempah*. Grind all the ingredients together in a blender (adding them in the order listed) to make a paste. Add a splash of water if necessary.

Heat the oil in a large flameproof casserole and stir-fry the *rempah* for about 5 minutes or until fragrant. Pour in the stock you've prepared and bring to the boil, then simmer for 30 minutes. Season with sugar, salt and pepper to your taste.

Put the cooked chunks of meat back into the soup and warm up, then dish the meat into serving bowls. Ladle generous amounts of soup into each bowl and garnish with fresh coriander, spring onions and crispy shallots. Add a squeeze of lime juice if you like and serve with rice.

SERVES 4, OR 6 AS A SIDE

1kg bone-in leg of mutton, cut into
   large chunks
3 carrots, peeled and cut into
   large chunks
3 celery sticks, cut into 6cm lengths
4 lemongrass stalks, woody ends
   trimmed off, bruised
1 large onion, peeled (left whole)
2 tablespoons cooking oil
1 tablespoon caster sugar
salt and white pepper

For the spice mix
3 pieces of star anise
1 cinnamon stick
5 whole cloves
6 cardamom pods
3 kaffir lime leaves

For the rempah
2 candlenuts or macadamia nuts
1 tablespoon coriander seeds,
   toasted
1 tablespoon cumin seeds, toasted
1 teaspoon fennel seeds, toasted
a 2.5cm piece of fresh turmeric,
   peeled (or use 2 teaspoons ground)
1 large onion, peeled and chopped
3 banana shallots, peeled and
   chopped
2 garlic cloves, peeled

To garnish
5 sprigs of coriander, chopped
2–3 spring onions, julienned
Crispy Shallots (see page 268)
lime quarters

"Mee Rebus"
Curried Noodle Soup

I prefer using fresh thick egg noodles for this soup, but thick or thin, fresh or dried are down to your preference.

SERVES 6

1 litre Beef Stock (see page 278),
  or Chicken Stock (page 279)
1kg meaty beef short ribs
700g sweet potatoes, peeled and
  diced into 3cm cubes
3 tablespoons cooking oil
600g egg noodles

For the rempah
1 candlenut or macadamia nut
a 3cm piece of fresh galangal, peeled
1 lemongrass stalk, tough outer
  leaves removed, and stalk roughly
  chopped
4 banana shallots, peeled and
  roughly chopped
4 garlic cloves, peeled
30 dried, moderately hot red chillies
  (use more or less to taste), soaked
  in lukewarm water
60g dried shrimps, soaked in
  lukewarm water
2 tablespoons Curry Powder
  (see page 267)
2 tablespoons fermented
  soya-bean paste
1 tablespoon salt
caster sugar, to taste

To garnish
Crispy Shallots (see page 268)
100g beansprouts, topped and
  tailed, blanched for 30 seconds
12 fresh green chillies, sliced
250g tofu puffs
6 hard-boiled eggs, peeled and cut
  in half
a bunch of coriander

Bring the stock to the boil in a large saucepan. Add the beef short ribs and bring back to the boil. Remove any scum that rises to the top, then reduce the heat to a minimum, cover and leave to simmer for 1–2 hours, depending on how big the short ribs are – you're aiming for the meat to fall off the bone neatly.

Meanwhile, steam the cubed sweet potatoes for about 10 minutes or until soft, then gently mash.

Grind all the *rempah* ingredients together in a blender (adding them in the order listed) to make a fine paste, adding a little water if needed. Set aside.

Heat the oil in a wok over a medium heat. Add the *rempah* and sauté, stirring constantly, until a richly coloured oil seeps from it. Set aside.

Remove any bones from the beef stock. Cut the beef into bite-sized pieces and return to the stock. Increase the heat under the pan to maximum and stir in the *rempah*. When it is fully incorporated, add the mashed sweet potatoes. Bring to the boil, then simmer on a low heat, stirring occasionally, until the gravy has reduced to a slightly thicker consistency. Add extra salt and sugar to taste.

Cook the egg noodles in a pan of boiling water until soft. Put the noodles into a serving bowl. Pour over the beef in gravy and garnish with crispy shallots, beansprouts, green chiilies, tofu puffs, eggs and coriander.

Babi Pongteh (or *Babi Pong Tay*) is a traditional Peranakan dish of braised pork in a fermented soya-bean sauce. Many family matriarchs of Peranakan Chinese households have cherished family recipes, handed down through the generations. It's traditionally a home-cooked meal, but was also a dish served at feasts and special occasions. In the early days a young Peranakan lady of marrying age was customarily required to demonstrate her cooking skills to her future in-laws by preparing a Peranakan delicacy like this dish. My dear in-laws had to settle for a tiramisu because I didn't have enough access to any ingredients to make anything elaborate!

Rinse the pork belly and drain, then cut into 2cm-thick slices. Set aside.

Soak the dried mushrooms in warm water for 30 minutes or until softened; drain. Cut off the stems, squeeze out excess water and set aside.

While the mushrooms are soaking, coarsely grind the shallots and peeled garlic in a blender and set aside. In a bowl, combine the fermented soya-bean paste, dark soy sauce, sugar, palm sugar and salt, and stir well to form a paste.

Heat up the oil in a wok over a medium heat. When hot, fry the shallot and garlic mixture with the cinnamon stick until fragrant. Add the fermented soya-bean paste mix next and stir-fry for a minute. Add the pork and fry briefly, stirring to coat evenly with the paste mixture. Add the water and cook over a high heat, stirring occasionally, until almost dry. Now pour in enough water to cover the pork and bring to a rapid boil for 5 minutes, giving the bottom of the pan a good stir.

Transfer from the wok to a heavy-based flameproof casserole. Add the unpeeled garlic cloves and rehydrated mushrooms. Cover with the lid, bring to a gentle simmer and leave to braise for 1–1½ hours. If the braising liquid reduces too quickly, add more hot water. If you prefer a thicker sauce or gravy, allow the braising liquid to reduce more.

When almost done, taste and add more sugar and salt if needed – be cautious with salt as the fermented soya-bean paste is heavily salted. Serve piping hot, with steamed rice.

SERVES 4

1kg pork belly (or trotters or
  shoulder), skinned
6 dried Chinese mushrooms
110g banana shallots, peeled
10 garlic cloves, 4 of them peeled
2 tablespoons fermented
  soya-bean paste
2 teaspoons dark soy sauce
1 tablespoon caster sugar
20–25g palm sugar, to taste,
  shaved or crumbled
½–¾ teaspoon salt, to taste
6 tablespoons cooking oil
1 cinnamon stick (about 8cm long)
150ml water

"Ngo Hiang"
Five-spice Pork Rolls

These are delicious pork sausage rolls spiced with Chinese five spice, wrapped very carefully in tofu skins then fried until crispy and served sliced on a platter. A dangerous combination when served with chilli and sweet soy sauce, our family could demolish a serving of this very quickly. Perfect to prepare ahead and makes the kitchen smell amazing when frying!

SERVES ABOUT 6

450g minced pork (preferably from the shoulder for its higher fat content)
200g raw prawns, peeled and finely chopped
1 large egg, lightly beaten
2 tablespoons light soy sauce
1 teaspoon fine sea salt
1 teaspoon white pepper
1 teaspoon five-spice powder
a 225g can water chestnuts, drained and roughly chopped
3 spring onions (green part), finely chopped
2 banana shallots, finely chopped

To finish
about 6 dried tofu sheets / skins, cut into 17.5 x 30cm rectangles
1 tablespoon cornflour, mixed with a little water to make a slurry
cooking oil
sweet dark soy sauce, for dipping

Mix together the pork and prawns in a large bowl. Add the egg, stirring to mix. In a separate bowl, stir together the light soy sauce, salt, white pepper and five-spice powder until smooth. Add to the pork and prawn paste and mix well. Mix in the water chestnuts, spring onions and shallots, distributing these ingredients evenly. Work the meat mixture well as you want it to bind together.

Lay a tofu skin rectangle horizontally on your work surface. Lightly pat the skin with a wet tea towel to dampen it. Arrange 3 heaped tablespoons of the spiced pork mix along the longer edge of the skin nearest to you, 1–2cm from the edges. Shape the meat into a slim sausage – it should be about 2.5cm thick and 3cm wide.

Starting with the edge closest to you and tucking in the short side edges as you go, roll up until the meat is fully enclosed within the skin. Using a pastry brush or your finger, use the cornflour slurry to 'glue' the edge of the tofu sheet and press to seal it. Place the roll, seam side down, on a plate. Repeat until you've used up all the pork mix.

Lightly grease a steamer tray, then steam the rolls for 8–10 minutes or until the skins turn translucent and the rolls feel firm. You could use a probe thermometer to check if the rolls are cooked – 73°C minimum. Remove the rolls and set aside on wire racks to cool.

At this point, you can divide the rolls into batches and freeze them for up to 3 months. To cook, thaw the rolls in an oven preheated to 180°C/160°C Fan/Gas Mark 4 for 10 minutes before frying as below.

To finish the rolls, heat a non-stick frying pan large enough to hold 2 rolls comfortably and add enough oil to cover the bottom of the pan thinly. Add the rolls, 2 at a time, and fry on a medium-high heat until the skins turn a crisp dark brown all over. Cool on kitchen paper or on a wire rack before slicing and serving. Wipe down the pan with kitchen paper before cooking the next batch. Slice the rolls into 2.5cm chunks and serve warm or at room temperature with sweet soy sauce.

daily
fare

It may seem as if we eat rich food every day, but that's hardly the truth. The complex dishes need time and attention, but those in this chapter are the ones that we make on a regular basis, day after day. None take longer than 1 hour from start to finish.

Mum would always ask us on the way to school, 'What do you fancy for dinner?' The question always made me feel a little guilty because I know how tiring it can be to go to work and then come home to cook for the family. But I think it was her therapy after being stuck in an office all day.

Our family meals would always be quite traditional, consisting of a soup, a vegetable dish (usually the Stir-fried Greens with Garlic on page 104) and a protein dish such as Sweet and Sour Pork (page 79) or Steamed Fish with Tomato, Silken Tofu and Ginger (page 72). The vegetable and protein dishes would be served family style, in big bowls on the table, with a small bowl of freshly steamed rice and individual bowls of a soup such as Watercress Soup (page 152) or Pork Rib Soup (page 163), which helped pick us up.

Egg Fried Rice

A few things will always make making egg fried rice extremely easy. Have cooled cooked rice to hand, typically leftover from the night before – then use a hot, seasoned wok to bring it together quickly so that you'll end up with a perfect egg fried rice that even Uncle Roger will approve of. The recipes on page 65 are some of my favourite variations on this classic egg fried rice recipe.

SERVES 4

3 eggs
600g cooked, cooled Thai
   jasmine rice
1 tablespoon cooking oil
2 tablespoons soy sauce, or to taste
1 tablespoon toasted sesame oil,
   or to taste
white pepper

Beat the eggs well in a bowl to mix the yolks and whites. Fork through the rice to separate the grains as much as you can.

Heat the cooking oil in a wok on a medium heat. Add the eggs and stir-fry until half cooked and still a little runny. Add the rice and continue to stir-fry until the rice is hot and mixed with the fully cooked egg.

Season to taste with the soy sauce, sesame oil and white pepper, then serve.

Mushroom and Spinach Fried Rice

This is a perfect way to get my son to eat his greens.

Before you fry the eggs, add the spinach, garlic and mushrooms to the oil in the wok and fry until they are cooked. Turn the heat up, then add the eggs followed by the rice as in the recipe on page 64. Stir vigorously until everything is cooked and thoroughly mixed. Add the spring onion and stir-fry until fragrant. Season as before.

SERVES 4

a handful of spinach, finely
   chopped
1 garlic clove, finely chopped
2 shiitake mushrooms, finely sliced
   or chopped
1 tablespoon cooking oil
3 eggs, beaten well
600g cooked cooled Thai
   jasmine rice
1 spring onion, finely sliced
soy sauce, toasted sesame oil and
   pepper, to season

Ham and Egg Fried Rice

This is a fridge-raid recipe when I'm totally out of time to worry about getting fresh ingredients. There is simply nothing wrong with frozen vegetables so don't feel guilty about using them.

Fry the ham and peas first, then follow the recipe on page 64.

SERVES 4

a 150g packet of cooked ham, diced
a handful of frozen peas (or cooked
   mixed vegetables)
1 tablespoon cooking oil
3 eggs, well beaten
600g cooked and cooled Thai
   jasmine rice
1 spring onion, thinly sliced
soy sauce, toasted sesame oil and
   pepper, to season

This dish is easily my sister Jane's favourite. She would guard the dish with a scowl if anyone reached for it on the dinner table. To make the dish successfully, use eggs and stock or water at room temperature – then when the mixture is steamed, it will set evenly throughout. If you use eggs straight from the fridge or cold liquid, there is a risk that the centre of the dish will be undercooked.

SERVES 4 AS A SIDE DISH

3 large eggs, at room temperature
about 300ml Chicken Stock
   (see page 279) or boiled water,
   at room temperature
1 teaspoon toasted sesame oil
1 teaspoon soy sauce
1 spring onion, finely sliced
salt and white pepper

Lightly beat the eggs in a bowl, ensuring the yolks are fully mixed with the whites. Slowly add the stock or water in the ratio of 1 part eggs to 2 parts water, stirring constantly to ensure an even mix. Add a pinch of salt and white pepper.

Strain the mixture into a heatproof bowl (choose one that will fit comfortably in your steamer – I use a bowl about 12cm in diameter) to remove any bubbles as well as any residual bits from the eggs or stock. Cover the bowl with clingfilm to prevent water dripping on to the mix during steaming.

Gently place the bowl in a steamer and steam over a low heat until the mixture is set. The time this takes will depend on the bowl you use, but it will be roughly 10 minutes in a shallow dish. Test the mixture by gently rocking the steamer: if the mixture moves, then continue to steam.

Remove the steamer from the heat. Leave the bowl in the steamer for a further 5 minutes, then carefully lift the bowl out using oven gloves or tongs.

Mix together the sesame oil and soy sauce, and pour over the steamed eggs. Garnish with spring onion.

"Tahu Goreng"
Fried Tofu Salad

The rich peanut sauce almost gives this tofu salad a meatiness to it so that it's a real stand out on its own. A definite family favourite.

SERVES 4

800g firm tofu
groundnut oil for deep-frying
1 cucumber, deseeded and sliced
200g beansprouts, topped and
    tailed, blanched for 30 seconds
50g unsalted peanuts, roasted and
    finely chopped

For the peanut sauce
2½ tablespoons shaved palm sugar
250ml boiling water
2½ tablespoons tamarind pulp
5 bird's eye chillies, chopped
    (optional)
3 garlic cloves, chopped
280g crunchy peanut butter
1 tablespoon *kecap manis*
    (sweet soy sauce)
1 tablespoon lime juice

To make the peanut sauce, mix the palm sugar with 125ml of the boiling water in a small saucepan and stir over a medium heat until the sugar has dissolved. Mix the hot palm sugar syrup with the tamarind pulp and leave for 10 minutes, then press through a fine sieve.

Blend the chillies (if using) with the garlic to make a smooth paste. Add the peanut butter, tamarind syrup, *kecap manis* and lime juice and blend to a chunky, thick but pourable sauce, adding more hot water if necessary.

Transfer to a small saucepan and bring to a simmer. Cook, stirring often, over a low heat for 4–5 minutes to allow the flavours to develop, adding a little more water if the sauce becomes too thick. Set aside to cool.

Pat the tofu dry with kitchen paper. Heat enough oil to cover the tofu in a wok (or fryer) over a medium heat to 175°C. Lightly fry the tofu until it is golden and crisp all over. Drain on kitchen paper to absorb the excess oil.

Put the fried tofu on to a serving plate. Carefully cut lengthways into 3–4cm-thick slices, then crossways to form cubes. Do this carefully to keep the original cake shape. Arrange some slices of cucumber and beansprouts around and over the tofu cake, then pour the sauce over all. Garnish with more slices of cucumber and beansprouts and the chopped peanuts.

Spicy Green Beans
with Chilli and Garlic

The traditional Nonya recipe for this dish calls for *kangkong* or water spinach. As here in England we do not usually have access to good-quality fresh Asian vegetables, I substitute French/green beans. Although I am fond of *kangkong*, I think this dish is actually better made with the beans because of their crunchy texture. It is also more affordable. If you want to make this vegetarian/vegan just omit the dried shrimps, *belachan* and pork floss.

Soak the dried shrimps and chillies in warm water for at least 10 minutes or up to 1 hour, then drain. If you don't want the dish to be too spicy, remove the seeds from the chillies, then place them in a blender with the soaked shrimps, garlic and shallots. Blend together to make a rough paste.

Heat the oil in a wok over a medium heat. Add the chilli-shrimp paste and stir-fry until aromatic, then add the *belachan* and stir for a couple more minutes to cook the paste out.

Turn up the heat slightly, add the green beans and give it all a good stir. Stir-fry for a couple of minutes. Add the water to help 'steam-cook' the beans and season with salt, then turn the heat down and continue cooking for 4–5 minutes or until the beans are tender (no more than 7 minutes in total).

Serve immediately with pork floss sprinkled on top, if using.

SERVES 2 AS A SIDE DISH

1 tablespoon dried shrimps
6 dried red chillies
3 garlic cloves, peeled
2 banana shallots, peeled
2 tablespoons cooking oil
2 teaspoons *belachan* (fermented shrimp paste)
250g green beans, trimmed and cut into 1.5cm pieces
2 tablespoons water
2 tablespoons pork floss (*rousong*), optional
salt

Steamed Fish with Tomato, Silken Tofu and Ginger

One thing I love about the UK is the wonderful access to top-quality fish. This dish brings out the best fresh flavour of a fish, and it's super versatile because you can use different fish. My favourite is sea bass, but any fish will do. Ask your fishmonger to scale and gut the fish for you, but leave the head on. Traditionally the fish cheek is served to the guest of honour or most elderly as this is the sweetest part of the fish. Luckily there are 2 sides, so 2 cheeks to go around. If you don't like fish on the bone, you can use a large fillet instead but adjust the cooking time accordingly (check it after 8 minutes). You'll need a steamer that is big enough for your fish.

SERVES 2

300g silken tofu, cut into slices or chunks
1 large tomato, sliced
2 spring onions, green parts finely sliced – reserve the white parts to garnish
1 whole sea bass, gutted
1 teaspoon fine sea salt
1 tablespoon dry vermouth
1 tablespoon rice wine (shaoxing or sake)
1 tablespoon water

For the dressing
1 tablespoon light soy sauce
1 tablespoon rice wine (shaoxing or sake)
1 tablespoon fish sauce
½ teaspoon white pepper

To garnish
2 spring onions, white parts finely julienned
20g root ginger, peeled and finely julienned
1 fresh, medium-hot, red Dutch chilli, deseeded and finely julienned (optional)
coriander leaves
Crispy Shallots (see page 268)

Heat up boiling water in your steamer. Choose a deep heatproof plate or tray that will fit into the steamer, and lay the tofu, sliced tomato and spring onion greens on the plate in one layer.

Cut 3 slashes in the fish on both sides, then rub the sea salt all over the fish. Place it on top of the tofu and tomato. Sprinkle the vermouth, rice wine and water all over the fish. Cover and steam for 12 minutes (8 minutes if using a fillet).

Check if the fish is cooked using a probe thermometer (73°C) or a fork to flake some of the flesh away from the bone: it shouldn't look translucent anywhere and should flake away nicely.

Carefully remove the plate from the steamer, taking care not to spill any of the juice. Spoon some of the fish juices from the plate over the fish.

Mix together all the dressing ingredients in a bowl, then pour over the fish. Check the seasoning. Sprinkle the garnish over the top and serve with plenty of rice.

Hokkien Prawn and Noodle Soup

The key to a perfect noodle soup is having a great stock. I always take care in removing the impurities that rise from the top of the bones when simmering.

Noodle soups make up every other meal we'd have at home because they contain so many nutrients, are cheap to make and, more importantly, are quick to put together.

To make the stock, bring the water to the boil in a stockpot or large saucepan. Add the stock bones, pork ribs, rock sugar, soy sauce and fish sauce. Simmer for 40 minutes. Skim off any foam or scum that rises to the top.

Add the pork fillet to the stock and simmer for 5 minutes. Add the prawns and cook for a further 2–5 minutes. Carefully remove the pork fillet and prawns and set aside. Strain the stock and set aside in a pan ready for reheating. Slice the pork fillet finely. Peel the prawns, devein and cut each in half lengthways.

Heat the oil in a wok or frying pan and fry the diced pork fat until crisp. Remove these crisps and set aside. Add the fish cake pieces to the rendered pork fat in the wok/pan and stir-fry for 3 minutes. Remove and drain on kitchen paper. Fry the shallots in the wok until they turn crisp. Drain.

Bring a large pan of water to the boil and blanch the noodles with the beansprouts and *kangkong* for 1 minute. Drain.

Divide the noodle mixture among the serving bowls and top with sliced pork, prawns, fish cakes, pork fat crisps, crisp-fried shallots, chillies and green garnishes. Top up with the soup stock and serve.

SERVES 6

250g pork fillet
500g large raw prawns
4 tablespoons cooking oil
250g pork fat, diced
3 Chinese fish cakes, sliced into thin pieces
2 banana shallots, sliced
800g fresh or soaked dried yellow noodles (Hokkien noodles or *eu mee*)
200g beansprouts, topped and tailed
200g *kangkong* (water spinach), cut into small pieces (or use leafy spinach)
5 fresh, medium-hot, red Dutch chillies, sliced
2 bunches of coriander, leaves picked and roughly chopped
2 spring onions (green part), chopped

For the stock
6 litres water
3 pork stock bones
500g pork ribs
a lump of Chinese rock sugar
2 tablespoons soy sauce
2 tablespoons fish sauce

Chicken Rendang

A really super easy supper that needs only a fraction of the cooking time of a beef rendang. It's not as dry as the beef version because the chicken cooks more quickly, meaning there is more delicious sauce.

SERVES 4–6

1 teaspoon fennel seeds
1 teaspoon cumin seeds
1½ tablespoons chilli powder
½ teaspoon ground turmeric
70g root ginger, peeled and
   julienned
15g garlic cloves, peeled
2 tablespoons cooking oil
150g banana shallots, finely sliced
6 chicken legs, split into 12–15
   thighs and drumsticks, on the
   bone and skin on
250ml canned coconut milk,
   coconut cream skimmed off the
   top and reserved
2 medium-sized tomatoes,
   quartered
salt

To garnish
a bunch of coriander, leaves picked
½ lime

Gently toast the fennel and cumin seeds in a dry pan for 1–2 minutes to release their fragrance. Grind the seeds with the chilli powder, ground turmeric, ginger and garlic in a blender to make a paste.

Heat the oil in a large flameproof casserole and fry the sliced shallots until golden brown. Add the spice paste and stir-fry over a low heat until fragrant, being very careful not to burn the paste. Add a touch more oil if necessary.

Add the chicken pieces and mix to coat with the spice paste, then add the thin coconut milk. Bring to the boil. Add the quartered tomatoes, cover the pan and simmer for 20–25 minutes or until the chicken is cooked through, stirring occasionally. Season to taste with salt. Add the coconut cream to help thicken.

Transfer to a serving bowl and garnish with coriander leaves. Squeeze lime juice over the top for acidity.

This is what I call a store cupboard dinner, and one that just sums up British-Chinese food culture – combining British food products, like HP and Worcestershire sauces, with Chinese flavours such as chilli sauce. The recipe makes enough for 12, which can be scaled down, but I find that everyone seems unable to stop eating it once they start. It's a really flexible dish – you can make it with 600g prawns instead of pork.

Mix together the bicarbonate of soda, salt, sugar, water and egg yolk in a bowl. Add the pork. Sprinkle the ½ tablespoon of cornflour over and mix well to coat the pork. Leave to marinate for at least 15 minutes.

Prepare the sauce by mixing all the ingredients together in a bowl. Mix the slurry ingredients in another bowl.

Heat the oil in a wok or heavy-bottomed pan to 170°C.

Working in batches, dredge the marinated pork cubes in extra cornflour and deep-fry until lightly golden and crispy, turning the pieces once in the oil to fry evenly. Remove carefully from the oil and place on kitchen paper on a tray to drain excess oil.

Fry the pork for a second time, for extra crispiness, but don't colour it too much. Transfer to a serving dish. Keep warm.

Pour most of the oil from the wok, leaving 2 tablespoons. Stir-fry the onion wedges. Pour in the sauce and bring to the boil, then turn down to a simmer. Whisk in the slurry a little bit at a time to thicken the sauce. Pour the sauce over the fried pork and garnish with the remaining ingredients.

SERVES 12

¼ teaspoon bicarbonate of soda
1 teaspoon salt
½ teaspoon caster sugar
1 tablespoon water
1 egg yolk
300g boneless pork shoulder, skin removed and excess fat trimmed off, diced into 2.5cm cubes
½ tablespoon cornflour, plus extra for dredging
groundnut oil for deep-frying

For the sauce
4 tablespoons caster sugar
1½ teaspoons salt
150ml water
1 teaspoon toasted sesame oil
4 tablespoons tomato ketchup
1 tablespoon Worcestershire sauce
1 tablespoon HP Sauce
2 tablespoons red wine vinegar
½ tablespoon chilli sauce

For the slurry
1½ tablespoons cornflour
2 tablespoons water

To garnish
1 large onion, cut into wedges
3 spring onions (green part), cut into 2.5cm pieces
1 fresh, medium-hot, red Dutch chilli, deseeded and julienned
1 cucumber, peeled, deseeded and finely sliced
1 tomato, cut into wedges

Aubergine and Pork Mince Stir-fry

This recipe makes a quick and easy dinner. The key is to cook the aubergine properly, making sure it is softened before adding the sauce. If you need to increase the cooking time for the aubergine, add more water to the wok to help it 'flash-steam' through.

SERVES 4

4 tablespoons cooking oil
400g minced pork
1 aubergine, cut into 5cm batons
about 150ml water
1 teaspoon cornflour, mixed with
    a little water to make a slurry
1 teaspoon white wine vinegar
½ teaspoon toasted sesame oil

For the sauce
3 tablespoons Chicken Stock
    (see page 279)
1 teaspoon miso paste
2 garlic cloves, finely chopped
¼ fresh red chilli, finely sliced
    (add more if preferred)
10 sprigs of coriander, leaves
    picked and stalks finely chopped
caster sugar
salt

To make the sauce, mix together the stock, miso paste, garlic, chilli and chopped coriander stalks in a bowl. Adjust the seasoning with sugar and salt to taste.

Heat the cooking oil in a wok on a medium-high heat. Add the pork mince and stir-fry until it starts to brown. Add the aubergine with the water and cook, stirring occasionally, for 3–4 minutes or until the aubergine has softened.

Add the sauce to the wok and stir through before adding the cornflour slurry, white wine vinegar and sesame oil and stirring again. (This is known as 'velvetting', to make the sauce rich with a velvet-like texture.) When the sauce has thickened, it's ready to serve, garnished with the remaining coriander leaves.

"Char Kway Teow" Wok-fried Noodles

CKT is super easy to make, affordable and really delicious. You can amp this dish up by using blood cockles, like the Singapore hawkers do, and cook this over charcoal to add the authentic aroma of *wok hei* (breath of the wok). Or make a simple version at home when you need to cook a fast but tasty dinner. Either way, this is a home-staple. We have our version with *kecap manis* because we have a sweet tooth, but you could leave this out. Use lard instead of oil when cooking the CKT, for a silkier texture. You'll need a very hot wok for this dish, so make sure you have everything prepared in advance and ready to go.

Rinse the *kway teow* noodles with lukewarm water, to help separate them. Drain well and set aside until needed.

Mix all the sauce ingredients together in a bowl.

To make the *rempah*, grind the chillies, garlic and shallots in a blender to make a smooth paste, and add a splash of water if necessary to help blend.

Heat 1 tablespoon of the oil in a wok over a medium heat, add the spice paste and fry, stirring constantly, for 2–3 minutes or until fragrant. Set the *rempah* aside on a plate.

Wipe the wok clean, then add the remaining oil and set over a medium heat. Add the finely chopped garlic and fry for 1–2 minutes or until it starts to colour. Turn up the heat to high, then add the prawns and Chinese sausages. Stir-fry until coloured and aromatic. Next add the beansprouts, Chinese chives, fried *rempah* and noodles. Mix well and fry for 5 minutes or until the vegetables are cooked and the noodles are coated.

Make a well in the middle and pour in the beaten eggs. Stir slowly to cook the egg, then mix the egg and sauce mixture with the noodles, lifting them up and stirring well to combine everything, being careful not to break up the noodles. Serve immediately.

SERVES 4

500g fresh flat rice noodles
   (*kway teow*)
4 tablespoons cooking oil
2 garlic cloves, finely chopped
200g peeled raw tiger prawns,
   deveined
2 Chinese sausages (*lap cheong*),
   about 80g in total, sliced
   diagonally
250g beansprouts, topped and
   tailed
2 Chinese chives, hard bottom
   of stem removed, cut into
   2.5cm pieces
2 eggs, beaten

For the sauce
4 teaspoons light soy sauce
1 teaspoon fish sauce
1 teaspoon salt
2 tablespoons dark soy sauce
2 tablespoons *kecap manis*
   (sweet soy sauce)

For the rempah
4 fresh, medium-hot, red Dutch
   chillies, roughly chopped
2 garlic cloves, peeled
5 banana shallots, roughly
   chopped

"Bak Chor Mee"
Minced Pork Noodles

I love, love, love this dish, not only because it contains crispy pork and chewy springy noodles, but it just hits so many notes on the palate and makes me happy. You can use thin noodles (*mee kia*) or wide noodles (*mee pok*). I don't normally add pork liver when I make it, but many Singaporeans do. I only leave out the liver because I want my son to eat with us. For the same reason I serve it with a tomato-chilli sauce instead of sambal tumis belachan. If you do want to include pork liver, be sure to get the freshest possible.

SERVES 4

200g minced pork
4 tablespoons light soy sauce
2 teaspoons ground white pepper
200g pork fat, cut into 5cm cubes
280g fresh egg noodles (*mee pok*)
green lettuce leaves, washed and
   left whole
500ml Chicken Stock
   (see page 279)
100g fresh pork liver, sliced thinly
   (optional)
2 spring onions, chopped
2 tablespoons Crispy Shallots
   (see page 268)
fine sea salt

For the braised mushrooms
12 dried shiitake mushrooms
1 tablespoon light soy sauce
1 tablespoon fish sauce
4 tablespoons oyster sauce
2 teaspoons caster sugar

For the sauce
5 tablespoons Chinese black
   vinegar
4 tablespoons light soy sauce
2 tablespoons Sambal Tumis
   Belachan (see page 262) or
   a tomato-chilli sauce
2 tablespoons Shallot Oil
   (see page 268)

The day before serving prepare the braised mushrooms and marinate the pork. Rinse the mushrooms under cold water, then place them in a large pan of water and bring to the boil. Remove from the heat. Add the remaining mushroom ingredients and set aside to soak for 30 minutes or until the mushrooms are plump and soft. Drain the mushrooms, remove the stems and slice thinly. Set aside.

In a separate bowl, mix the minced pork with the light soy sauce and white pepper. Leave to marinate overnight.

Fry the pork fat in a large pan over a medium heat until the liquid fat is fully rendered. You'll be left with small crispy bits. Drain these crisps on kitchen paper to absorb excess fat and season with fine sea salt; set aside. Pour 4 teaspoons of the rendered pork fat into a bowl (discard any excess).

To make the sauce, add the black vinegar, soy sauce, sambal tumis belachan and shallot oil to the rendered pork fat in the bowl. Mix together. Divide this sauce among the serving bowls.

Blanch the noodles in a pan of boiling water until cooked but still al dente. Drain well, shaking off any excess water. Divide among the bowls along with some lettuce leaves.

Bring the stock to the boil. Put the minced pork in a fine metal sieve, or a noodle basket (which I prefer), and blanch in the stock for 2–3 minutes, or until just cooked. Lift the sieve out and add the cooked pork to the noodle bowls, breaking it up with a fork. Now repeat with the pork liver, if using, blanching it in the stock until just cooked.

Garnish the bowls with the sliced braised mushrooms, cracklings, spring onions and crispy shallots. Ladle the hot stock over the top or serve in separate bowls.

I love the combination of the two noodles in this fried noodle dish. We'd eat this mid-week because my mother would make a giant wok full of it when she managed to get hold of fresh seafood, and it would be enough for us to enjoy for breakfast and lunch the next day. I love to squeeze lots of fresh lime juice over the top to bring out the seafood flavours.

Take the skin off the pork belly. Remove the excess pork fat and dice it, then reserve.

Bring the water to the boil in a large saucepan. Add the pork belly, prawns and squid. After 2 minutes, lift out the prawns and squid and set them aside. Continue boiling the pork for 5 minutes before lifting it out. Skim any foam from the surface of the stock in the pan, then set aside.

Cut the pork belly into strips. Peel and devein the prawns, then cut each in half lengthways. Cut the squid into rings.

Heat up a wok and fry the diced pork fat until crisp; set aside. There should be about 4 tablespoons of rendered fat left in the wok.

Add the crushed garlic to the rendered fat and fry until it starts to turn brown. Push it to one side, out of the fat, to prevent it from burning, then crack the eggs into the hot fat and stir to break up the yolks. Add the noodles, vermicelli and beansprouts and pour in about 100ml of the stock. Stir for 1 minute, then cover and leave to cook for a further 2 minutes.

Remove the lid and stir-fry for 3–4 minutes. Add more stock, just enough to moisten, and continue frying for 5 minutes. Add the pork belly, prawns and squid and stir until the mixture is cooked, adding more stock as needed so everything is coated with sauce.

Add the fish sauce and chives and stir once. Garnish with the crisp pork fat dice and serve with chillies or sambal belachan and fresh lime.

SERVES 4–6

a 250g piece of pork belly
1 litre water
150g raw tiger prawns
150g squid (prepared for cooking)
6 garlic cloves, crushed
3 eggs
500g dried or fresh yellow noodles (Hokkien noodles or *eu mee*)
150g dried rice vermicelli (*bee hoon*), soaked
150g beansprouts, topped and tailed
2 tablespoons fish sauce
100g Chinese chives, cut into 3cm lengths

To serve
fresh chillies or Sambal Belachan (see page 263)
lime

super
quick
meals

It's tough trying to achieve a level head while running a business, doing errands and chores, keeping a little one entertained and also making a healthy balanced dinner each day. Of course, time escapes you. So, here is a collection of quick, easy recipes that will only get faster the more you practise and make them.

I found that slicing or chopping the 'holy trinity' of basic aromatics – garlic, ginger and shallot – together saves time. Add a touch of chilli, sambal or tamarind juice and you're nearly there with the spice base for a dish. At home, we always had a plastic tray of condiments such as oils, sambals and sauces near at hand. With a well-stocked pantry and a few fresh ingredients, healthy and varied dinners can be produced in a flash.

Asparagus with Wok-fried Egg, Coconut and Sambal

When I was approached for the role of Head Chef at Pidgin, the test for me was to cook something that was different and seasonal (it was April at the time so plenty of asparagus around). Also, as it was 10am, the dish needed to be 'brunch' style. Since I've always got a jar of sambal in my pantry, this recipe was a perfect fit.

SERVES 4

500g asparagus
4 tablespoons cooking oil
4 free-range eggs
sea salt and white pepper

To garnish
2 teaspoons Sambal Tumis
   Belachan (see page 262)
2 tablespoons coconut
   cream powder

Trim the woody ends from the asparagus. Thinly peel the stalks from just below the tip down. Add the spears to a pan of salted boiling water and blanch for 1 minute (if your asparagus spears are thick, then 2 minutes at most).

Using a slotted spoon, lift the asparagus out of the boiling water and into an ice-bath to stop it cooking. (Alternatively you can cool the asparagus under cold running water.) Once cooled, place the spears on a tray and pat dry. Season with a pinch of sea salt and set aside.

Heat up some of the cooking oil in a wok over a high heat (you want enough oil in the wok to almost shallow-fry the eggs). Cook the eggs one at a time: crack one egg into a ramekin or small bowl, then slip gently into the hot oil, which should immediately start to bubble around the egg. Season the yolk with salt and pepper, then use a Chinese spatula to carefully flick hot oil over the egg to cook the white.

When you no longer see any translucent egg white, carefully transfer the egg to a tray lined with kitchen paper or absorbent cloth. Continue to shallow-fry the remaining eggs. If you run low on oil, just top it up and wait for it to heat up.

Serve the hot eggs with the asparagus, ½ teaspoon of sambal per serving and a dusting of the coconut cream powder across the top.

My mother would always have a bag of dried shrimps
somewhere in the depths of the fridge drawer, and a cupboard
with a selection of fats and oils, so stir-fried cabbage was a
staple of our dinnertime meals.

Discard any fibrous or discoloured outer leaves from the greens,
or cut out the hard core of the cabbage. Finely shred the
vegetables.

Add the lard or oil to a wok set over a high heat and swirl the fat
around so the wok is well coated. Add the shrimps and stir-fry until
crisp, then remove carefully with a slotted spoon and set aside.

Heat the wok until it is smoking, then add the greens or cabbage
and stir-fry briskly until just barely cooked but still a little crispy.
Return the shrimps to the wok along with the soy sauce and sugar
and mix well. Check the seasoning (the shrimps can be salty), then
serve with a drizzle of shallot oil.

SERVES 4

400g spring greens or white
    cabbage
4 tablespoons lard or cooking oil
4 tablespoons dried shrimps
1 tablespoon light soy sauce
1 tablespoon caster sugar
1 tablespoon Shallot Oil
    (see page 268)

Beansprout Salad

Beansprouts are very common now in supermarkets and an affordable way to bulk out a meal or even to have on their own with noodles or rice. Be sure to look for fresh, crispy white beansprouts – they shouldn't be dull in appearance or slimy.

SERVES 4 AS A SIDE

3 tablespoons cooking oil
5 garlic cloves, sliced
½ brown onion, thinly sliced
1–2 fresh, medium-hot, red Dutch
  chillies, deseeded and finely
  sliced
3 tablespoons oyster sauce
½ teaspoon toasted sesame oil
1 tablespoon rice wine (shaoxing
  or sake)
300g beansprouts, topped and
  tailed
2 spring onions, finely sliced
¼ teaspoon white pepper

Heat the oil in a wok over a medium heat and stir-fry the garlic, onion and chillies for about 1 minute.

Add the oyster sauce, sesame oil and rice wine, and mix well before adding the beansprouts and spring onions. Increase the heat and stir-fry quickly for 2–3 minutes. Season with the white pepper and serve immediately.

Crispy Salt and Pepper Tofu with Chilli

Here is a really nice dish to get children involved in food prep.
I put the flour mix in a large resealable bag and add the tofu,
then get Riley to give it a good shake – and pray that we don't
end up with cornflour tofu mess all over us and our kitchen floor.

First remove as much liquid as possible from the tofu by pressing
it overnight or patting well with kitchen paper. The tofu needs
to be dry so the flour coating will stick and give a good crunchy
texture.

Dice the tofu into small bite-sized chunks, about 2.5cm. Place in
a bowl or bag with the flour mix and toss or shake to coat the tofu
evenly. Transfer the tofu to a tray, ready to cook. Combine the
spice mix ingredients in a bowl and set aside.

Heat up a wok with the oil over a medium heat and gently fry the
garlic slices. When the garlic starts to colour, remove it carefully
from the oil using a slotted spoon or strainer and set aside.

Turn up the heat and add the tofu, in batches if necessary. Fry
until it turns a lovely golden colour and the edges are really
crispy, moving the tofu around in the wok to colour all edges.
Return the garlic slices to the wok along with the chillies and
spring onions.

Place the crispy tofu on kitchen paper to remove any excess oil,
then season immediately with the spice mix, turning the tofu to
make sure it is well coated. Taste to check the seasoning and add
a little more spice mix if you want it quite punchy.

SERVES 4

a 700g block firm tofu,
   drained well
3 tablespoons cooking oil
1 garlic clove, thinly sliced
2 fresh, medium-hot, red Dutch
   chillies, deseeded and thinly
   sliced (or more if you prefer)
2 spring onions, thinly sliced

For the flour mix
4 tablespoons cornflour
1 tablespoon rice flour

For the spice mix
1½ teaspoons salt
1½ teaspoons caster sugar
½ teaspoon white pepper
a pinch of five-spice powder
a pinch of ground Sichuan pepper

Stir-fried Greens with Garlic

In the 1990s we lived outside of London, so we had to go into London's Chinatown to buy fresh Asian vegetables. That was always a special trip because we could also gorge on all the sweet treats in the Chinese bakeries. Now you can find *pak choi* or *choi sum* in most supermarkets. It's still worth the effort to find an Oriental supermarket though as vegetables there will cost a fraction of the price.

SERVES 4

300g *choi sum* (or *pak choi, kai lan* or leafy spinach)
2 tablespoons cooking oil
2 garlic cloves, finely chopped
1 teaspoon salt
1 teaspoon caster sugar
1 tablespoon dry vermouth
1 tablespoon rice wine (shaoxing or sake)

Discard any discoloured leaves from the greens and trim off any hard woody ends. Cut the stems from the leaves, keep both separate, and wash well; drain. Cut the stems in half lengthways if they are thick (as on *choi sum*).

Add the oil to a wok set over a high heat and swirl the oil around so the wok is well coated. When the oil is smoking add the stems from the greens and stir-fry briskly, using a Chinese spatula, for a couple of minutes. If there's a loud sizzle from the stems and oil then the heat is just right.

Next add the garlic and stir well, then add the leaves from the greens and keep stirring until just wilted,. Add the salt and sugar followed by the vermouth and rice wine to season. If the greens are looking a little dry, or need to steam more, add a splash of water to the wok. Check the seasoning and serve immediately.

Variations:
Stir-fried vegetables with oyster sauce and mushrooms
Stir-fry the stems with finely sliced oyster mushrooms or fresh shiitake mushrooms and replace the vermouth and rice wine with 2 tablespoons oyster sauce.

Stir-fried spinach
Leafy spinach is best for this, but you can use baby spinach although you won't get a lot of yield out of it. Trim any stems off 300–400g spinach, wash at least 3 times in fresh water and drain well. Heat up the oil in the wok, add the spinach, stir and toss, then add salt and serve. You can also do this with peashoots (my mum's favourite), beansprouts, mangetout or even turnip tops.

Another way to flavour stir-fried spinach is to add a crushed garlic clove to the wok just before the spinach. When the greens have begun to wilt, add a splash of water – about a tablespoon – to help the spinach steam more, then add 1 tablespoon oyster sauce and 1 teaspoon each caster sugar and salt. Toss to mix and serve.

Prawn and Pineapple Curry

This is my mum's favourite curry as it is fast and easy to cook. It is based more on the Thai/Malaysian style of curry, as it doesn't actually contain any curry spices but is super fragrant, sour and spicy. These days fresh raw prawns in shell are readily available and reasonably affordable. The same goes for fresh pineapple. For this dish, you should choose a relatively green pineapple so that it gives the dish a bit of a sour kick.

Grind the *rempah* ingredients together in a blender (adding them in the order listed) to make a paste. Add a splash of water to help it grind if necessary.

Heat the oil in a pan, add the *rempah* and stir-fry until fragrant. Add the water and half the coconut milk and stir well, then bring to the boil.

Add the prawns, pineapple and chillies and cook for 10 minutes on a low simmer. Add a pinch of sugar to taste and a pinch of salt (sugar will give this curry a little sweetness plus an extra hit of umami). Stir in the rest of coconut milk and bring to the boil.

Taste and add more salt if necessary. Garnish with some chopped coriander and serve on steamed rice.

SERVES 4

4 tablespoons cooking oil
500ml water
a 450g can coconut milk, shaken to mix the contents
500g large raw prawns, peeled and deveined
½ small pineapple, peeled, cored and cubed
2 fresh green chillies (jalapeños), cut in half and deseeded
2 fresh, medium-hot, red Dutch chillies, cut in half and deseeded
caster sugar to taste
chopped coriander to garnish
salt

For the rempah
2 candlenuts or macadamia nuts
a 2.5cm piece of fresh turmeric, peeled (or 2 teaspoons ground turmeric)
1 lemongrass stalk, dry end removed, stalk roughly chopped
4 banana shallots, peeled and roughly chopped
4 garlic cloves, peeled
1 tablespoon *belachan* (fermented shrimp paste)

"San Bei Ji"
Three Cup Chicken

My mum is like a magpie – she will try out any recipe that she has read about or tasted. This is her adaptation of a Taiwanese recipe, although the dish itself originated in Jiangxi province and was taken to Taiwan by the Hakka people. Three Cups is the literal translation of *San Bei*, which originates from the ingredients used in making the sauce i.e. 1 cup toasted sesame oil, 1 cup soy sauce and 1 cup Chinese rice wine (shaoxing). My mum doesn't follow the exact rule and changed the recipe to suit our family's taste.

SERVES 6

1 tablespoon cooking oil
a 5cm piece of root ginger, peeled and cut into 8 slices
6 garlic cloves, lightly crushed but whole
2 tablespoons toasted sesame oil
12 chicken thighs (skin on)
a handful of Thai basil leaves, plus extra to garnish
1 fresh, medium-hot, red Dutch chilli, sliced into strips (optional)
1 teaspoon cornflour, mixed with a little water to a slurry (optional)

For the sauce
2 tablespoons light soy sauce
1 tablespoon dark soy sauce
3 tablespoons mirin (Japanese sweet cooking wine)
1 tablespoon *kecap manis* (sweet soy sauce – omit if you don't like it too sweet)

Heat the cooking oil in a sauté pan. Add the ginger slices and cook for a few seconds, then add the garlic and sesame oil. When the ginger and garlic are almost brown add the chicken pieces. Cook over a medium heat until the bottom of each chicken thigh is lightly golden. Flip over and continue to cook until both sides are lightly golden.

Add all the sauce ingredients. Cover the pan with a lid and simmer for 5 minutes. Remove the lid and add the Thai basil leaves and chilli. Stir in the cornflour slurry, if using to thicken the sauce, and continue simmering on a low heat until the chicken is cooked through. Remove any large pieces of ginger or garlic if preferred. (I leave them in, but it's personal choice.)

Garnish with more Thai basil and serve warm with steamed rice.

"Ma-Po Tofu"
Tofu with Minced Pork

This is my mum's version of the Sichuanese dish *Mapo Doufu*. It's perfectly inauthentic, and a fusion of different ingredients, ideas and styles coming together. I leave out the chilli, pepper and Gochujang paste when I cook this for Riley, then add it in after I've scooped out a portion for him to enjoy.

Heat the oil in a wok, then stir-fry the garlic, spring onion, ginger and crushed fermented black beans for about 3 minutes or until fragrant. Add the hot bean paste and cook, stirring, for 1 minute or until aromatic. Mix in the chilli flakes and Sichuan pepper.

Add the minced pork. Continue to stir to cook the pork, breaking it up with a spoon. When the meat changes colour, add the rice wine, water, caster sugar, salt and soy sauce to season, followed by the tofu. Simmer for 3 minutes over a low heat.

Mix together the cornflour and water until smooth, then slowly pour into wok, stirring but being careful not to break up the tofu too much. Once mixed well and slightly thickened, garnish with the julienned spring onion and serve.

SERVES 6

3 tablespoons cooking oil
1 teaspoon chopped garlic
1 tablespoon chopped spring onion
  (white part)
1 teaspoon peeled and chopped
  root ginger
2 teaspoons crushed fermented
  black beans or black bean sauce
1 tablespoon Gochujang paste (hot
  chilli paste) or hot bean paste
1 teaspoon dried chilli flakes
2 teaspoons ground Sichuan
  pepper
450g minced pork
1 tablespoon rice wine (shaoxing
  or sake)
240ml water
½ teaspoon caster sugar
½ teaspoon salt
1 tablespoon soy sauce
500g soft tofu (or firm tofu if you
  want more texture), cut into
  2.5cm chunks
2 tablespoons julienned spring
  onion (green part)

For the slurry
1½ teaspoons cornflour
1 tablespoon water

"Mee Sua"
Fine Rice Noodle Soup with Pork Meatballs

My son Riley quickly took to this super fast noodle dish when introduced to solid foods. I usually make it with chicken stock, or you can use water with a low-salt chicken stock cube so it's suitable for children. Add fish sauce or fine sea salt at the end to your own taste.

SERVES 4

240g minced pork
1 teaspoon light soy sauce
½ teaspoon white pepper
2 tablespoons cooking oil
2 garlic cloves, finely chopped
500ml Chicken Stock
   (see page 279)
2 bundles (about 100g) of dried
   fine rice vermicelli (*mee sua/
   misua*)
4 eggs (optional)
fish sauce
salt

Combine the minced pork, light soy sauce and white pepper In a small bowl, then shape into small meatballs, around the size of a walnut.

Heat the oil in a saucepan. When it's hot, add the garlic and sauté until golden and fragrant. Pour in the chicken stock and bring to a gentle boil.

Drop the meatballs into the stock, then add the vermicelli. Simmer until the noodles are soft and the meatballs are cooked through (5–8 minutes). If using, add the eggs, one by one, to poach gently, then season to taste with fish sauce and salt.

Serve immediately because the rice vermicelli will absorb the liquid quickly.

This quick and delicious beef stir-fry is a staple dish for us at dinnertime at home. You can omit the chilli and dried chilli flakes if you're cooking for little ones, which is what I do for my son, Riley. As with all stir-fries, have your ingredients measured and prepped ahead, because the cooking time is very short.

Stir the marinade ingredients together in a bowl. Add the beef and mix in well with the marinade.

Add 3 tablespoons of the oil to a wok set over a high heat and swirl the oil around to coat the wok. When it is starting to smoke, add the beef and stir-fry briskly, separating the pieces using a Chinese spatula. When the pieces are separated and still a little pink, remove them from the wok and set aside.

Add the remaining oil to the wok, then add the ginger and garlic. Allow them to sizzle for a few seconds to release their fragrance. Tip in the red pepper and fresh chilli, if using, and stir-fry until hot.

Return the beef to the wok and give everything a good stir, then add the chilli flakes. When all is hot and fragrant, add the spring onions and remove from the heat. Stir in the sesame oil, check the seasoning and serve.

Variation: Stir-fried venison
Venison is a very healthy alternative to beef, as it is rich in iron, potassium and zinc and is very lean. Just replace the beef in the recipe above with 250g venison fillet, cut into strips, and add a splash of stock at the end to prevent the stir-fry from being too dry.

SERVES 4

- 250g boneless beef rump, sliced into bite-sized pieces
- 4 tablespoons cooking oil
- 1½ teaspoons finely chopped root ginger
- 2 teaspoons finely chopped garlic
- 1 red pepper, cut into bite-sized pieces similar to the beef
- 1 fresh, medium-hot, red Dutch chilli, deseeded and finely chopped (optional)
- 2–4 teaspoons dried chilli flakes, or to taste
- 2 spring onions (green part), finely sliced
- 1 teaspoon toasted sesame oil

For the marinade
- 1 teaspoon rice wine (shaoxing or sake)
- ¼ teaspoon salt
- ½ teaspoon light soy sauce
- ¾ teaspoon dark soy sauce
- 1½ teaspoons potato flour
- 1½ teaspoons water

Beef Ho Fun

Here is a quick, simple wok-fried noodle dish that's very versatile.
I couldn't get enough of it when I finished late at the restaurant.
I would reheat a big bowl of it to eat with some pickled chillies
on the side.

SERVES 4

300g lean boneless beef fillet
  or rump
4 tablespoons cooking oil
5 garlic cloves, finely chopped
600g fresh, or rehydrated dried,
  flat rice noodles (*kway teow*)
½ white onion, thinly sliced
300g beansprouts, topped
  and tailed
100g Chinese chives or spring
  onions, cut into 2.5cm pieces

For the marinade
1 ½ tablespoons soy sauce
2 teaspoons rice wine (shaoxing
  or sake)
1 teaspoon caster sugar
1 teaspoon cornflour
1 teaspoon toasted sesame oil
1 teaspoon vegetable oil

For the stir-fry sauce
2 tablespoons dark soy sauce
2 tablespoons *kecap manis*
  (sweet soy sauce)
1 tablespoon vegetable oil

Slice the beef thinly against the grain. Combine the soy sauce, wine, sugar and cornflour for the marinade in a small bowl. Add the beef and mix well. Leave to marinate for at least 20 minutes, then add the sesame and vegetable oils.

Mix the ingredients for the stir-fry sauce in a small bowl and set aside.

Heat the cooking oil in a wok over a medium heat and fry the garlic until crispy and golden. Remove the garlic and set aside in a bowl.

Turn up the heat to high and, when hot, add the beef and its marinade. Stir-fry the beef until the colour changes – about 30 seconds. Remove the beef from the wok and set it aside along with the fried garlic.

Next, add the rice noodles along with the stir-fry sauce mixture and stir-fry over a high heat, constantly tossing and moving the noodles, for about 4 minutes or until they appear lightly browned. Add the onion, beansprouts and chives, and stir-fry until well combined.

Lastly add the beef and garlic back to the wok and toss for about 30 seconds until well combined and hot. Serve immediately.

summertime

One thing we have always loved about living in the UK is the seasons. Summer was definitely our favourite. We'd be out in the parks or in the garden, pretending to be helping Dad with the gardening and lighting up the barbecue to have dinner outside. Mum would prepare the ingredients and Dad would cook it all. Now my forte as a chef is barbecue, and I take the helm with the tongs.

In Singapore some of the street hawkers specialise in barbecue dishes. They have a long barbecue and cook delicacies such as Barbecue Belachan Fish, wrapped up in aromatic banana leaves (see page 131), or Otak Otak (page 43) or even satays. When visiting Singapore we order satays by the dozens, of mutton, chicken or beef, and sit outdoors for hours eating them with buckets of beers until the mozzies start to pinch. Satays to me are the most satisfying bite from a barbecue because you can slather them with a sticky, rich peanut sauce or have them plain with a good squeeze of lime juice (calamansi lime, if you have it). Pure happiness on a stick.

This collection of recipes is a mix of dishes from a traditional barbecue in Singapore and others that I've developed since becoming a chef.

Barbecue Sweetcorn with Miso Koji Butter

We love fresh sweetcorn, and so whenever our farm shop has these in season, I always light up the barbecue and get these on. The sweetness from the corn matches perfectly with the sweetness from the miso and the saltiness from the *koji*. Don't worry if you can't find *shio koji*, just use a little extra salt to season.

Prepare the barbecue (or heat the oven grill).

Blanch the sweetcorn whole in salted boiling water for 1 minute, then place in an ice-bath to stop it cooking any more. Drain and pat dry.

In a small bowl, mix together the butter, *shio koji*, miso and chilli until smooth and evenly blended. Alternatively, pulse together in a small food processor. Gently melt the butter in a saucepan.

Place the sweetcorn on the barbecue rack, directly over the hot coals, to colour lightly on all sides, then use a pastry brush to liberally coat with the *miso koji* butter. Continue cooking until the sweetcorn is nicely blistered all over. Give it one final brush of the butter, then serve.

SERVES 4

4 sweetcorn cobs, husks and silk removed
175g unsalted butter, at room temperature, cubed
1 tablespoon *shio koji* paste
½ tablespoon white miso
1 fresh, medium-hot, red Dutch chilli, deseeded and finely chopped

Coal-roasted Aubergine with Crispy Chilli Oil

For me, no barbecue is complete without this super easy side. Make it when you've finished cooking the meats, but have still hot embers going in the barbecue. Be sure to prick the aubergines at least once or twice before roasting otherwise they could explode when they cook, which is a hot mess no one wants. If you don't want to make your own chilli oil, I recommend one from Lao Gan Ma brand, called spicy chilli crisp.

SERVES 4 AS A SIDE

4 aubergines
juice of 1 lemon
Crispy Chilli Oil (see page 264)
small bunch of coriander, roughly
   chopped
salt

Pierce each aubergine at least twice, in different places, with a fork or sharp knife.

When you have finished barbecuing the meats, lift the grills off the barbecue and place the aubergines in the hot embers. Cook, turning every now and then, for 5–10 minutes or until soft. (Alternatively, you can roast the aubergines in the oven preheated to 200°C/180°C Fan/Gas Mark 6. First blister the skin of the aubergines over a gas flame, holding them with tongs, then place them on a baking tray and roast in the oven for 20 minutes or until soft.)

Transfer the coal-roasted aubergines to a tray and cover with cling film. Leave for 5–10 minutes or until cool enough to handle.

Carefully peel the skins off the aubergines and discard. Put the aubergine pulp into a bowl and break it up into pieces using a spoon. Season with lemon juice and salt, then drizzle plenty of crispy chilli oil over the top. Garnish with coriander and serve.

Barbecue Lettuce with Thai Dressing

Sometimes I want something sharp and fresh, especially when I'm cooking a barbecue of rich meats. This 'Thai' dressing is just perfect. Nonya cuisine can be very fragrant and rich, and the acidity from this dressing makes a really refreshing change. Use it on meat such as chicken wings or on vegetables. Add chilli to your taste or omit if you are feeding children. I like to add freshly sliced green or red chilli at the end so I don't have to make 2 versions.

SERVES 4 AS A STARTER

2 baby Gem lettuces, cut in half
   lengthways
1 fresh green chilli, sliced
   (optional)

For the dressing
100g soft light brown sugar
50ml water
zest of 6 limes
150ml freshly squeezed lime juice
150ml fish sauce (I like Mega Chef
   brand)
20g garlic paste
20g ginger paste

To garnish
a small bunch of coriander,
   roughly chopped
a small bunch of mint or Thai basil,
   leaves picked and torn
50g roasted peanuts, roughly
   chopped

Prepare the barbecue (or you can use a hot ridged cast-iron grill pan).

To make the dressing, put the brown sugar and water in a small saucepan and bring to the boil, stirring until the sugar has dissolved and a syrup forms. Set aside to cool.

Combine the remaining dressing ingredients in a bowl and whisk together, or pulse in a small food processor. Check the seasoning: you might want to add more lime for sharpness or more fish sauce for saltiness. Stir in the sugar syrup.

Place the lettuce halves cut side down on the barbecue rack, directly over the hot coals and grill for 5–10 minutes (depending on the heat) or until well charred and hot. Don't move the lettuce around while it's grilling.

Once well charred, remove the lettuce from the heat and place on a tray cut side up. While the lettuce is still warm, cover it with the dressing and add the sliced chilli (if using) and garnishes, making sure you push these in between the lettuce layers. Serve immediately. If you have any leftover dressing, keep it in an airtight container in the fridge and use within 2 days.

For us this is a firm favourite in the summer whenever we fire up the barbecue. The intense aroma of the grilling fish and banana leaves takes me back to the hawker centres in Singapore, with such warm memories of eating out with my family. If you don't have a barbecue, you could easily cook this dish in a hot ridged grill pan. I usually use skate wings for this dish, similar to the stingray they use in Singapore. However, if I can get hold of a good flat fish, like Dover or lemon sole or even splashing out on turbot, these all will work perfectly too. Just ask your fishmonger to gut and dress (trim) your fish for you.

Grind the *rempah* ingredients together in a blender, adding them in the order they are listed, to make a paste. Heat up a wok with the cooking oil and stir-fry the paste for 5–6 minutes or until it is fragrant. Set aside to cool.

Pat the banana leaves dry, then lightly coat with some oil. Place a piece of fish on one piece of leaf. Spread the cooked *rempah* evenly on both sides of the fish, then place another piece of banana leaf on top. Secure by weaving through wooden cocktail sticks or bamboo skewers. Prepare the remaining parcels in the same way.

Heat up the barbecue. Place the fish on the grill to cook for 8–10 minutes, turning over very carefully after 4–5 minutes. To make the turning easier, you can place the parcels in a fish grid. Grill the fish until the flesh will pull away cleanly from the bones.

If you don't have access to a barbecue, heat a cast-iron ridged grill pan and cook the fish for about 10 minutes on each side (cooking time will vary depending on the size of your fish).

To serve, place the parcels on plates and carefully remove all skewers or sticks. Peel off the top layer of leaves. Serve the fish with the shallots, sambal and lime to squeeze over plus plenty of napkins.

SERVES 2

1 tablespoon cooking oil
2 large banana leaves, soaked in warm water to soften, then trimmed to 4 pieces the size of the fish pieces (large enough to cover)
vegetable oil for coating
1 large skate wing, skinned and cut in half (so you end up with 2 pieces), thick bone at the top removed

For the rempah
2 lemongrass stalks, dry ends removed, roughly chopped
4 banana shallots, roughly chopped
6 fresh, medium-hot, red Dutch chillies, cored and roughly chopped
¼ teaspoon ground turmeric
1 tablespoon toasted *belachan* (fermented shrimp paste)
1 tablespoon fish sauce
juice of 2 limes (calamansi limes if you can get hold of them)
1 tablespoon caster sugar

To serve
2 banana shallots, finely sliced
2 tablespoons Sambal Tumis Belachan (see page 262)
1 lime, cut in half

Barbecue Prawns
with Sambal Chilli

We always have a jar of sambal tumis belachan in the fridge, and so this is a simple but impressive dish to put together because the *belachan*, fermented shrimp paste, is a perfect pairing with the barbecue king prawns.

Prepare the barbecue (or heat a ridged cast-iron grill pan).

One at a time, place the prawns on a chopping board, curved back upwards, and holding firmly, run a knife from the back of the head along the back to the tail. This will help the prawns cook more quickly.

Put the prawns into a bowl with the sambal and mix well. If the sambal is a little dry, add the cooking oil to help coat the prawns evenly.

Place the prawns on the barbecue rack, directly over the hot coals, and grill for up to 10 minutes, turning them over halfway through, until they are all cooked. Use tongs to remove them from the grill to a plate.

Serve with slices of lime on the side. (The heads and shells are great to keep and use for stock if you wish to make Hokkien *mee* dishes.)

SERVES 4

600g raw king prawns (in shell)
2 tablespoons Sambal Tumis Belachan (see page 262)
1 tablespoon cooking oil, if needed
lime

Barbecue Chicken Wings with Sticky Taré Sauce

Always a winner when there's a hint of sunshine outside. Serve these with plenty of wet wipes at hand. They go incredibly well with Smacked Cucumber (see page 272) or Beansprout Salad (page 98).

SERVES 4

8 large free-range chicken wings
300ml Taré Sauce (see page 276)
100g molasses
1 lemon

For the chicken wing brine
1 litre water
90g sea salt
30g muscovado sugar
50g honey
mixed herbs – thyme, rosemary,
    bay (optional)
freshly ground black pepper

To make the brine, put all the ingredients into a large pan and bring to the boil, then leave to cool. Once the brine is cool add the chicken wings and leave to brine in the fridge for 2 hours.

Meanwhile, put the taré sauce into a saucepan and stir in the molasses. Simmer to reduce to a sticky sauce. Think of a runny honey texture.

Prepare the barbecue. You want a temperature of about 200°C, which will be when the flames have died down and the coals are ashy grey with red hot interiors.

Remove the wings from the brine and dry thoroughly with kitchen paper. Grill the wings on the barbecue to get a little colour all over, then baste the wings liberally with the taré sauce. Continue grilling, turning the wings and regularly basting with the sauce. Keep the wings moving on to different spots on the barbecue because the sugars in the taré glaze will colour quickly. Use a probe thermometer to check if the wings are cooked through: they should be at 73°C minimum.

Add a good squeeze of lemon across the chicken wings before serving.

Duck Heart Satay with Sticky Glaze

Duck hearts are very cheap and really tasty glazed with this sticky demi-glace, which is a heavily reduced beef stock. Prepare the glaze ahead, as it will keep well in the fridge or even freezer. Use home-made or fresh, shop-bought beef stock but avoid stock cubes, as these tend to have a high salt content. Ask your local butcher to source duck hearts for you if you struggle to find them in the supermarket.

First, soak 10 bamboo skewers in water for at least 6 hours.

To make the sticky glaze, put the red wine into a saucepan and reduce on a medium heat until thick and syrupy. Add the remaining ingredients and reduce on a medium heat until rich and thick, occasionally skimming the foam off the top. Keep an eye on the glaze when it is about 85 per cent reduced to prevent it from over-reducing and burning.

Thread the duck hearts on to the soaked skewers and set aside on a tray ready to barbecue.

Prepare the barbecue. (Alternatively preheat the oven grill to hot or use a hot frying pan.)

Place the skewers on the barbecue grill, directly over the hot coals, and grill for about 2 minutes on each side or until well coloured and charred. The meat should be medium rare/pink; if overcooked, the hearts will be really chewy.

Brush the duck hearts with the glaze and season with a good squeeze of lime juice. Serve immediately.

MAKES 10 SKEWERS

250g duck hearts, sinews trimmed
1 lime, cut into quarters

For the sticky glaze (demi-glace)
60ml red wine
1.3 litres beef stock
10g glucose syrup
1 teaspoon salt
½ teaspoon Curry Powder
  (see page 267)

Chicken Satay

You can use chicken breasts instead of thighs for this recipe if you prefer; however, I find that breast has a tendency to dry out more quickly. My favourite part of the chicken for satay is the small 'oysters' found on the underside of a carcass, but this is such a small amount you won't end up with many satays. Skinless boneless thighs are perfect for portioning for satays and if you choose to brine the chicken first, it will be even more moist.

MAKES 20 SKEWERS

500g skinless boneless
    chicken thighs
chopped cucumber
chopped red onion
compressed rice cakes

For the brine (optional)
1 litre water
90g table salt
150g caster sugar
2 tablespoons runny honey

For the marinade
3 slices of fresh galangal, peeled
a 3cm piece of fresh turmeric,
    peeled (or 1 tablespoon
    ground turmeric)
4 lemongrass stalks, chopped
10 banana shallots, chopped
2 garlic cloves, peeled
1 tablespoon fennel seeds
1 tablespoon ground cumin
1 teaspoon salt
1 tablespoon caster sugar

For the peanut sauce
200g skinned roasted peanuts
4 large dried red chillies, soaked
    in water overnight
3 tablespoons cooking oil
200ml Tamarind Juice (see page
    269), made with 1 tablespoon
    tamarind pulp
1 tablespoon caster sugar
salt

First make the brine (if using) as you need it to be cooled completely before you add the chicken. Heat up the water, salt, sugar and honey in a pan until the sugar and salt have dissolved. Remove from the heat and set aside to cool.

Cut the chicken into small 3cm cubes and place in the cooled brine. Leave for at least 6 hours, then drain.

Grind together all the ingredients for the marinade in a blender, adding a splash of water to help blend if necessary. Mix well into the chicken pieces. Leave the seasoned chicken in the fridge overnight. Soak 20 bamboo skewers in water for at least 6 hours or overnight.

The next day, thread the chicken on to the skewers and set aside on a tray ready to cook. Reserve leftover marinade.

To make the peanut sauce, follow the method on page 143, using the leftover marinade from the chicken. Add a little splash of water or extra tamarind juice if it gets too dry and starts to catch in the pan.

Prepare the barbecue or preheat the oven grill.

Barbecue the skewers over an indirect heat (i.e. not directly over the hot coals) for about 4 minutes on each side or until nearly cooked through, then shift them over direct heat and flames to get more colour on them for about 1 minute. A probe thermometer should register 73°C. Alternatively, grill indoors for 10–15 minutes, turning over halfway.

Serve immediately with peanut sauce, chopped cucumber and onion, and rice cakes.

There are some days that are simply perfect. For me, that would have to be a Sunday with my family, at our local hawker in Bedok, eating a pile of satays with a big bucket of beers and chatting about life and ambitions. Mutton satay is my favourite because I love the flavour, but beef, lamb and chicken work really well too (if using beef, just add ½ teaspoon chilli powder to the marinade). Marinate the meat and soak the skewers overnight to prevent burning.

Cut the mutton into strips and then into small 3cm pieces. Grind all the marinade ingredients together in a blender to make a fine paste, adding a splash of water if necessary. Mix with the mutton and leave to marinate overnight.

Meanwhile, soak 20 bamboo skewers in water for at least 6 hours, or overnight.

The next day, thread the meat on to the skewers and set aside on a tray ready to barbecue. Reserve the leftover marinade.

To make the peanut sauce, put half the peanuts into a food processor and pulse a couple of times until the nuts are roughly chopped; set aside. Put the rest of the peanuts into the processor and blend until finely ground. Set aside.

Drain the soaked red chillies and put into the blender with the reserved marinade paste. Grind until smooth. Heat up the cooking oil in a wok over a medium heat and fry this spice paste, stirring constantly, until fragrant. Next add the tamarind juice and the finely ground and coarse peanuts and simmer for about 30 minutes, stirring occasionally. Season with sugar and salt. You want a rich golden sauce with a pourable consistency, so thicken by reducing more or thin with water as needed.

Prepare the barbecue (or preheat the oven grill). Place the skewers on the barbecue over an indirect heat (i.e. not directly over the hot coals) and grill for about 4 minutes on each side, then shift them over direct heat and flames to get more colour and char them for about 1 minute. A probe thermometer should register 73°C. (Alternatively, grill in the oven for 10–15 minutes, turning halfway.)

Serve immediately with the peanut satay sauce in a bowl and chopped cucumber, red onion and rice cakes.

MAKES 20 SKEWERS

300g boneless mutton shoulder

For the marinade
2 slices of fresh galangal, peeled
4 lemongrass stalks (white parts)
10 banana shallots, peeled
2 garlic cloves, peeled
2 tablespoons ground coriander
1 tablespoon ground cumin
½ teaspoon ground turmeric
1 teaspoon salt
2 teaspoons light soy sauce
120g caster sugar

For the peanut sauce
200g skinned roasted peanuts
4 large dried red chillies (such as Arbol), soaked overnight
3 tablespoons cooking oil
200ml Tamarind Juice (see page 269), made with 1 tablespoon tamarind pulp
1 tablespoon caster sugar
salt

To serve
1 cucumber, deseeded and roughly chopped
1 red onion, roughly chopped
compressed rice cakes

"Char Siu"
Honey Roast Pork

Traditionally pork fillet or tenderloin is used for Char Siu but I love using the neck end fillet because it has more fat running through it and so is a lot more juicy, whereas the fillet or tenderloin, being so lean, can dry out a lot more quickly. This is one of Riley's favourites as the meat is so sweet. I serve it in lettuce cups so he can pick it up, wrapped in the lettuce, to eat. Voilà! I've got him to eat salad without really knowing it. You can also just serve it straight onto freshly steamed rice, or toss it through some cooked noodles with greens.

Char Siu is known for its pink-coloured meat, which comes from the artificially coloured hoisin sauce normally used in the marinade. I prefer to use a good-quality hoisin sauce that doesn't contain colouring. If yours is the same but you want that pink blush, add a little dash of beetroot juice.

Bring the caster sugar, honey and water to the boil in a medium saucepan, stirring until the sugar and honey have dissolved. Pour into a large bowl to cool.

Put the sesame paste, hoisin sauce and soya-bean paste in a blender and pulse until smooth. Rub this paste generously over the pork and leave to marinate for at least 6 hours or ideally overnight in the fridge, uncovered.

Preheat the oven to the highest setting – mine goes to 230°C/210°C Fan/Gas Mark 8.

Scrape excess marinade off the pork and reserve it for later. Set the pork on a rack over a foil-lined roasting tray and roast for 15–20 minutes or until the pork starts to blister and colour well. Turn the oven down to 150°C/130°C Fan/Gas Mark 2 and continue roasting until the meat is around 73°C inside (check with a probe thermometer), basting with the reserved marinade after 20 minutes. The total cooking time will be between 40 minutes and 1 hour.

Place the pork in the cooled sugar syrup and leave to 'candy' for at least 2 hours.

When ready to serve, preheat the oven grill to medium. Lift the candied pork out of the sugar syrup on to a grill tray. Grill, turning constantly, until the meat starts to turn crispy and get colour and is warmed through. Carve to serve in the lettuce cups with pickles, or straight on freshly steamed rice or cooked noodles.

SERVES 4–6

250g caster sugar
2 tablespoons runny honey
125ml water
125g sesame paste
125g hoisin sauce
125g fermented soya-bean paste
2kg pork neck end fillet, skin and
    membrane trimmed off

To garnish
4 baby Gem lettuces, separated
    into leaf cups
Nonya Mixed Vegetable Pickle
    (see pages 274–275), optional

pick me ups

I feel there's a tendency for people to associate Chinese food with unhealthy, greasy or gluttonous take-aways. Yes, it's true that a lot of take-away restaurants have given Chinese cuisine a bad reputation by cutting corners to make an extra buck. However, Chinese food is actually more helpful to good health than many people know. In Chinese medicine shops you find dried flowers, herbs and roots that all have their own special properties. A lot of soups are made with these ingredients, and they are often served alongside main meals.

If we ever needed a proper pick me up – from the daily stresses of school, or running a business – we'd happily finish every drop of a bowl of herbal soup. If one of us were ill, or had a tummy upset, my mum would make congee because it's light on the stomach but still nutritious. If one of us craved congee, she would always ask 'What's wrong with you? Are you sick?' and then insist we have a shot of ginseng syrup. These herbal recipes still always cheer me up when I'm emotionally, physically or mentally down.

Watercress Soup

This soup is lean and healthy and is especially good in the summertime when watercress is readily available. Make sure to get fresh crisp watercress, preferably the bunched stuff. The soup is quick and easy to make and is good enough to serve just with plain rice or as part of a meal.

SERVES 2

50g minced pork
½ teaspoon soy sauce
toasted sesame oil
160g watercress
600ml Chicken Stock
  (see page 279)
30g lean boneless pork, sliced
½ teaspoon fish sauce, or to taste
100g soft tofu, cut into small cubes
Crispy Shallots (see page 268)
salt and white pepper

Mix the minced pork with the soy sauce, a sprinkle of pepper and a few drops of sesame oil in a small bowl. Form into little balls and set aside.

Clean the watercress well, discarding any old stems and yellow leaves. Set aside.

Put the chicken stock into a saucepan and bring to the boil. Add the sliced lean pork followed by the minced pork balls. Simmer for 5–6 minutes to cook the pork.

Season to taste with fish sauce, then add the watercress and soft tofu. After a further 1 minute of cooking, remove from the heat.

Sprinkle the crispy shallots on top of the soup and serve.

This is a simple yet delicious soup. You can add a bit more Chinese *choi sum* and make it a side dish, or add noodles and serve it as a meal on its own.

Start by making the wonton filling. Put all the ingredients, except the prawns, in a bowl and mix together by hand for 5 minutes. You want to make sure that the pork and seasonings are thoroughly combined. Mix in the chopped prawns until evenly incorporated.

To make each wonton, take a wonton skin and put about 1 teaspoon of filling in the middle. Wet the edges of the skin with water, then bring the 2 opposite corners together to form a triangle, trying to remove as much air from the wonton as possible (to prevent it from bursting open later on). Press the edges together to seal. Dust the bottom of the wonton with a tiny bit of cornflour to prevent them from sticking together.

Continue making wontons like this – you should be able to make about 3 dozen, depending on how generous you are with the filling.

Bring the salted water to the boil in a saucepan, then turn the heat down to medium. Add the wontons one at a time to the water. Don't rush and don't crowd the pan, cook in batches if you need to. Once a wonton is cooked, it will float to the surface, around 4–5 minutes. Scoop out the cooked wonton and place in cold water for 10 seconds. Lift out and set aside. Continue until all your wontons are cooked.

To complete the soup, bring the chicken stock to the boil in a large pot, then turn the heat down to medium. Season with salt, pepper and soy sauce to taste. Add the *choi sum* or lettuce, then add the cooked wontons, dropping them gently into the soup. Take care not to stir hard as you don't want to break the delicate wontons. Ladle into bowls. Alternatively, I find it easier to put the wontons into bowls and ladle the stock into the bowls. Garnish each with chopped spring onions and a drop of sesame oil.

SERVES 4, OR 6 AS A SIDE

½ pack wonton skins/wrappers (readily available in Chinese supermarkets)
2 litres salted water
2 litres Chicken Stock (see page 279)
soy sauce
choi sum or lettuce, shredded
spring onions, chopped
toasted sesame oil
salt and white pepper

For the filling
200g minced pork (with 10% fat)
¾ teaspoon salt
½ teaspoon caster sugar
½ teaspoon toasted sesame oil
a good pinch of white pepper
1 tablespoon rice wine (shaoxing or sake)
2 teaspoons corn or groundnut oil
1 tablespoon water
½ teaspoon cornflour, plus extra for dusting
170g peeled raw prawns, chopped

Chicken Macaroni Soup

This is a staple lunch dish at home, sometimes made on the rare occasions when we have leftover Hainanese Chicken Rice (see page 196). If using leftovers, simply cook the pasta, heat up the leftover chicken stock for the soup, season well and garnish with the coriander and crispy shallots. You can add sliced chilli for a fresh kick of heat, which is most welcome if you are tired!

SERVES 6

1 chicken, about 1.4kg
2.5 litres water
1 teaspoon black peppercorns
1 teaspoon salt
½ teaspoon white pepper
1 teaspoon light soy sauce
½ teaspoon toasted sesame oil

For the pasta
4 litres water
1 tablespoon salt
400g macaroni pasta

To garnish
a small bunch of coriander,
   leaves picked
Crispy Shallots (see page 268)
sliced fresh red chilli (optional)
6 eggs, soft-boiled for 7 minutes,
   peeled and cut in half

Put the chicken into a large pot and cover with water. Add the black peppercorns. Bring to the boil, partially covered, then turn the heat down and simmer, covered, for 30 minutes or until the chicken is cooked. Skim the foam from the surface of the stock.

Lift out the chicken into a colander (reserve the stock in the pot) and place it under cold running water to stop the cooking. Let the chicken cool down completely, then remove the skin and take the meat off the carcass and bones, tearing it into shreds. Set the meat aside.

Return the carcass to the stock in the pot and simmer for another 30 minutes. Season the stock well with the salt, white pepper, light soy sauce and sesame oil. Strain the stock through a sieve into another pot, ready to reheat for serving.

Meanwhile, cook the pasta. Bring the water to the boil in another saucepan, add the salt and then the pasta and cook according to the packet instructions until al dente. Drain in a colander and run cold water over the pasta to stop the cooking.

To serve, divide the cooked pasta among the bowls, top with shredded chicken and ladle over the seasoned chicken stock. Garnish with coriander leaves and crispy shallots, as well as the sliced chilli, if using, and the soft-boiled eggs.

Whenever I used to feel run down, or under pressure from
exams or work, or even motherhood, my mother would always
tell me I needed to take ginseng. This ginseng soup is an age-
old brew that Chinese wives and mothers lovingly prepare for
their family to strengthen them physically and mentally. I tend
to cook it when my family is feeling rather lethargic. I love to
eat this with some steamed rice and stir-fried vegetables.

Put the chicken thighs (or poussins), ginseng and peppercorns
in a large saucepan and cover with the cold water. Cover the pan
and bring to the boil, then turn down to a simmer and cook for at
least an hour or until the chicken meat is tender and about to fall
off the bones.

Add the salt and soy sauce. Ladle the soup and chicken into
bowls. If serving young children, try to remove as many of the
chicken bones as possible.

SERVES 4

700g chicken thighs (or 2 whole
  poussins)
4 knobs of ginseng
1 teaspoon black peppercorns
1.5 litres cold water
½ teaspoon salt, or to taste
125ml dark soy sauce

Sweetcorn and Spare Rib Soup

Near my parents' house, there is a farm where you can 'pick your own' – depending on the season, this could be sweetcorn, strawberries, plums or anything else they have on offer at the time. It is a great family experience that I recommend for any age. Riley just loves running through the sweetcorn fields and is really excited to see us cook it at home. This is my sister's favourite soup. I must add that this soup isn't the sticky, thick sweetcorn soup that you get in UK Chinese restaurants, but is fresh and light, perfect as a side soup or dish or even as a meal itself.

SERVES 4

700g pork spare ribs
2 sweetcorn cobs, husks and
    silk removed
1 carrot, peeled and cut into
    6–8 chunks
2 litres water
soy sauce
salt

Put the pork ribs in a large pot, cover with water and bring to the boil. Blanch for 4–6 minutes, then drain and rinse the ribs. This helps remove any impurities to get a clear soup.

Put the ribs back into the clean pot and add the sweetcorn, carrot and water. Bring to the boil, then turn down to a slow simmer. Cook for 1½–2 hours depending on the size of the pork ribs.

About 30 minutes before the end of cooking, take out the sweetcorn and set aside to cool. Cut the sweetcorn kernels off the cob. Return both cobs and kernels to the pot and continue to simmer until the cooking time is up.

Remove the sweetcorn cobs. Season to taste with salt and a dash of soy sauce. Ladle into soup bowls and serve.

"Bak Kut Teh" Pork Rib Soup

This Chinese herbal soup is perfect for the colder months. *Bak kut teh* literally translates as 'meat bone tea' – 'tea' because the spice mix is usually packed in a sachet like a tea bag, which is steeped with the pork ribs before they are simmered until the meat falls off the bone and is mouth-wateringly soft. You can buy the spice mix in sachets as part of the pack of *bak kut teh* herbs, but be warned that most contain a lot of MSG or salt. If you can source the pack of herbs, put them into a muslin bag and take it out before serving. You can then add back as much or as little of the herbs to your soup as you wish. I like to bulk out the pork with goji berries, shiitake mushrooms and tofu puffs.

Bring the water to the boil in a large pot. Put the contents of the pack of *bak kut teh* herbs, except for the spice sachet, in a muslin bag. Add the *dong gui* to the bag too, then tie the top closed.

When the water comes to the boil, add the muslin bag, spice sachet, *yok chok*, dates and mushrooms. Leave on the heat.

Heat the oil in a large frying pan. Add the garlic and pork ribs. Sear the ribs for about 3 minutes. Stir in the soy sauce. Carefully transfer the pork ribs and garlic to the large pot. Add the rock sugar. When the liquid comes back to the boil, season with salt. Reduce the heat to low and leave to simmer, uncovered, for about 1½ hours.

Add the tofu puffs, tofu-skin knots and goji berries. Simmer for a further 30 minutes.

Discard the muslin bag and the spice sachet. Add the white pepper and check the salt. Serve with steamed rice and cut chillies in soy sauce.

SERVES 6

2.5 litres water
a pack of *bak kut teh* herbs, rinsed and drained
3 slices of *Angelica sinensis* (*dong gui*, Chinese angelica), rinsed and drained (optional)
10g *yok chok* (Solomon's seal rhizome)
10g red or black dates
12 dried shiitake mushrooms, soaked until soft, rinsed and stems removed
2 tablespoons vegetable oil
1 bulb of garlic, cloves separated (unpeeled)
1kg meaty pork ribs or 1 whole back of ribs
2 tablespoons dark soy sauce
10g Chinese rock sugar (or granulated sugar)
12 small tofu puffs, cut in half
6 tofu-skin/sheet knots
30g dried goji berries, rinsed and soaked for 10 minutes, then drained (optional)
½ teaspoon white pepper
Chilli and Soy Sauce (see page 262) to serve
salt

Beef Short Rib Soup
with Carrot and Onion

Every now and then, we trek to New Malden to visit a Korean restaurant called 'Jingogae' because their lunch deals are incredibly good value and very tasty. This soup dish is inspired by the Korean 'Galbitang' and is really cheap to make. You can bulk it out with sweet potato noodles if you wish.

SERVES 4

4 beef short ribs, cut into smaller
   pieces (ask the butcher to
   do this)
1 tablespoon *shio koji* paste
   (optional)
1 brown or white onion, peeled
500g mooli (white radish), peeled
   and cut into 5cm chunks
1 large carrot, peeled and cut into
   5cm chunks
2 bundles of sweet potato noodles,
   or mung bean noodles (optional)
2 teaspoons salt, or to taste

Place the beef short ribs in a large saucepan and add enough water to cover by 2.5cm over the beef. Bring to the boil, then skim the foam off the top and turn down to a very low simmer. Add the *shio koji*, if using, and the onion. Cover the pan and leave to simmer for 3 hours or until the bone pulls away easily from the meat. (Alternatively, use a pressure cooker and cook for about 1½ hours.)

Add the mooli and carrot and simmer gently for a further 30 minutes or until the vegetables are soft.

In the meantime, if using the noodles, put them into a bowl and cover with hot water. Leave to soak for about 15 minutes or until softened. Drain and add to the soup just before serving.

Check the seasoning of the soup, adding salt to taste (*shio koji* is very salty), then serve in bowls with or without rice, as you prefer.

When we used to ask 'Muuuuummmm, what's for dinner?', it meant we were hungry, but we were also super curious. I have to admit that cabbage rice was never in my top ten; however, it's one of those dishes that once I start eating it, I can never stop because it's so moreish and delicious. The name 'Cabbage Rice' just doesn't do it justice, so you could call it 'Mushroom, cabbage and prawn rice'. Riley is going through a 'rice only' eating phase, so this is a great way to sneak vegetables into his diet.

Put the pork into a bowl with the marinade ingredients and mix well. Leave to marinate for at least 30 minutes.

Meanwhile, soak the Chinese sausage in boiling water for a few minutes, then remove the skin and dice into small chunks. Put the rice into a rice cooker without any liquid and set aside.

Drain the mushrooms, reserving the soaking water, and remove the hard stems. Squeeze excess water from the mushrooms, then cut each into thin strips. Remove the dried shrimps from their soaking water and set aside with the mushrooms. Mix the shrimp water with the mushroom water to make up enough liquid to cook the rice. If needed, add extra cold water.

Heat the oil in a wok over a medium heat and sauté the soaked shrimps for 2–3 minutes, then add the shallots and sauté until fragrant. Add the Chinese sausage, shiitake, pork belly and marinade and continue to sauté for a few minutes. Add the salt along with the mushroom and shrimp water mix, and bring to the boil.

Pour the mixture on top of the rice in the rice cooker, without stirring. Lay the cabbage on top, then set the rice cooker to cook as normal.

Once the rice is cooked, add the dark soy sauce and sesame oil plus a good sprinkle of white pepper and stir in, mixing well.

Serve garnished with spring onion and crispy shallots and with a good-quality Chinese chilli oil on the side.

SERVES 4

50g pork belly, skinned and diced
1 Chinese sausage (*lap cheong*)
500g Thai jasmine rice
8 dried shiitake mushrooms,
   soaked until soft
50g dried shrimps, soaked
   until soft
3 tablespoons cooking oil
1 tablespoon sliced shallots
1 teaspoon salt
½ white cabbage, cored and sliced
   into 1cm strips
1 tablespoon dark soy sauce
1 tablespoon toasted sesame oil

For the marinade
½ teaspoon white pepper
½ teaspoon salt
½ teaspoon toasted sesame oil
1 teaspoon light soy sauce

To garnish
1 spring onion (white part), sliced
2 tablespoons Crispy Shallots
   (see page 268)

Fish Congee

For my family, congee is the ultimate comfort food, and there are a few recipes for congee on the following pages. The best rice for this dish is broken rice but any rice, apart from basmati, will do. Instead of mackerel you can use sea bass or cod.

SERVES 4–6

4 fillets of mackerel, skinned and thinly sliced
240g rice (preferably broken rice), soaked in cold water for a few hours and drained
2.8 litres water or Fish Stock (see page 277)
a 2cm slice of root ginger, peeled and julienned
salt and white pepper

To garnish
2 spring onions, finely sliced
Crispy Shallots (see page 268)
1 tablespoon toasted sesame oil

Season the fish slices with a pinch of salt and pepper. Set aside.

Put the rice and water or fish stock into a large pot and bring to the boil. Reduce the heat to low and simmer, covered, for 1¾ hours or until it has the consistency of porridge. Stir frequently during the last 30 minutes of cooking. The congee will continue to thicken as it stands, so thin with water if necessary.

Add the ginger and season with salt. Stir, then remove from the heat. Add the fish and mix in well. Leave to sit for 5 minutes so the residual heat in the rice can cook the fish.

To serve, ladle the congee into bowls and garnish with spring onion, fried shallots, a pinch of ground white pepper and sesame oil.

Chicken Congee

This is my mum's go-to meal if any of us are feeling low or ill, because it's easy to digest and light on the stomach. We love adding different ingredients into our bowls depending on our moods. For a rich congee, our family favourite is to crack an egg yolk into the bottom of each bowl before ladling the rice porridge on top. The heat of the porridge will cook the egg yolk and when you mix it through the porridge it creates the loveliest colour and flavour! The best rice for this dish is broken rice or jasmine, but any, apart from basmati, will do.

To make the stock, put the chicken thighs into a large pot with enough water to cover. Add the ginger and spring onions. Bring to the boil, then simmer uncovered for about 30 minutes, skimming away any scum that rises to the surface as the chicken cooks. Remove the pan from the heat, and take the chicken out carefully. When it has cooled down completely, tear the meat into shreds. Set the chicken meat aside.

Put the chicken bones and skin back into the stock and simmer for another 30 minutes. Strain the stock into a large bowl. You should have about 2.3 litres of stock. If you have more than this, don't worry (you can just cook longer after adding the rice later on), but if you have less add water to make the quantity.

Pour the stock into the cleaned pot and add the rice. Bring to the boil and stir, then reduce the heat to low and simmer, covered, for about 1¾ hours or until the consistency of porridge. Stir frequently during the last 30 minutes of cooking. Season well with salt. Congee will continue to thicken as it stands, so thin with water if necessary.

To serve, ladle the congee into bowls and top with the shredded chicken, spring onions, sesame oil, fried shallots and a pinch of white pepper.

SERVES 4–6

240g rice (preferably broken rice), soaked in cold water for a few hours and drained

For the stock
6 chicken thighs (bone in)
3 slices of root ginger, peeled
3 spring onions, smashed gently

To garnish
2 spring onions, finely sliced
1 tablespoon toasted sesame oil
Crispy Shallots (see page 268)
salt and white pepper

MAKAN

Crab Congee

This is made in the same way as the Chicken Congee on page 171, but using a crab stock instead of chicken stock. If you don't want to handle live crabs you can substitute fish stock for the crab stock, and used picked crab meat. The best rice for this dish is broken rice or jasmine but any, apart from basmati or wild rice, will do.

SERVES 4–6

240g rice (preferably broken rice), soaked in cold water for a few hours and drained

For the stock
2 live brown crabs
3 litres water, or 2.3 litres Fish Stock (see page 277)
3 slices of root ginger, peeled
3 spring onions, smashed gently
salt

To garnish
2 spring onions, finely sliced
Crispy Shallots (see page 268)
1 tablespoon toasted sesame oil
white pepper

To make the crab stock, dispatch the crabs or ask your fishmonger to do this. Place them in a pot with the water (or enough to cover), ginger and spring onions. Add some salt. Bring to the boil, then simmer for about 12 minutes. Take the crabs out carefully (reserve the water) and cool in an ice-bath. When the crabs are completely cooled down, crack the shells and pick out the white and brown meat. Return the shells to the pot of water and simmer for a further 30 minutes.

Meanwhile, pick carefully through the white meat to remove any bits of shell or cartilage. Blend the brown meat in a food processor until smooth, then pass through a very fine sieve. Mix the white and brown meat together and season with salt. Set aside.

Strain the crab shell stock into a large bowl. You should have about 2.3 litres of stock; if less than this, add more water. If too much, just cook longer after adding the rice later on.

Return the stock (or the fish stock) to a clean pot and add the rice. Bring to the boil and stir. Reduce the heat to low and simmer, covered, for about 1¾ hours or until the consistency of porridge. Stir frequently during the last 30 minutes of cooking. Congee will continue to thicken as it stands, so thin with water if necessary. Season well with salt.

To serve, ladle the congee into bowls and top with the crab meat, spring onions, crispy shallots, a pinch of white pepper and sesame oil.

"Tauk Yu Bak"
Braised Pork Belly

Literally translated, this means soy sauce pork as it's braised slowly in soy sauce until its soft and tender. It's a very comforting one-pot dish, and always hits the right note when the weather is turning cold.

Heat the oil in a heavy-bottomed pot and lightly brown the garlic and ginger. Add the chunks of pork and sear them on all sides. Add the soy sauce and stew for 5 minutes, stirring constantly to prevent burning or sticking. Ensure that the pork is well coated with soy sauce.

Add the water and bring to the boil, then lower the heat to medium, cover and braise the pork for 45 minutes or until it is cooked through and tender.

Add the tofu puffs and hard-boiled eggs and simmer, uncovered, for a further 10 minutes.

Add salt to taste. Continue to simmer on the lowest heat for 10 minutes, or until the gravy reaches your desired consistency. Serve hot with steamed white rice.

SERVES 4

2 tablespoons cooking oil
4 garlic cloves, crushed
a 2–3cm piece of root ginger, peeled and crushed
500g pork belly, skinned and cut into small chunks
4 tablespoons dark soy sauce
1.5 litres water
6 tofu puffs
4 hard-boiled eggs, peeled and left whole (optional)
salt

Braised Chicken with Black Fungus and Shiitake

This dish comes from my maternal grandmother who is Cantonese and a great cook. The Chinese believe that many of their ingredients have medicinal properties, and dishes are cooked as much for these as well as being nutritious and delicious. Black fungus, which is believed to prevent blood clots, is used in lots of Chinese dishes. It doesn't have much flavour on its own but when cooked properly it is very tasty with a silky texture. As with most of my mum's cooking, she just adds ingredients according to her taste rather than following a set recipe (*agak agak* – the Malay word for guesstimate). For this one, she would use either chicken wings or thighs as she thinks that the dark meat is tastier. I completely agree with her.

SERVES 4

6 skinless boneless chicken thighs, cut into strips
125g dried lily buds, soaked until soft and drained
1 tablespoon cooking oil
4 garlic cloves, smashed with a knife
5 thick slices of root ginger, peeled
10 pieces of dried shiitake mushrooms, soaked until soft, drained and cut into slices
80g dried black fungus mushroom, soaked until soft, drained and cut in half if too big
250ml water
2 tablespoons rice wine (shaoxing or sake)
1 tablespoon oyster sauce
1 teaspoon cornflour, mixed with a little water to make a slurry (optional)
salt

For the marinade
2 teaspoons dark soy sauce
2 teaspoons toasted sesame oil
2 teaspoons rice wine (shaoxing or sake)
a pinch of caster sugar
a pinch of white pepper

Put the chicken meat into a bowl and add all the marinade ingredients, along with a pinch of salt. Stir well to coat the meat. Leave to marinate in a cool place for an hour. Meanwhile, remove the stems from the lily bulbs and tie into a knot.

Heat up a wok with the cooking oil and fry the crushed garlic and ginger slices until they turn light brown but not burnt. Add the marinated chicken strips and stir-fry until brown on all sides.

Add the shiitake and black fungus mushrooms and the lily stems. Stir-fry for 30 seconds, then add the water, rice wine, oyster sauce and a pinch of salt. Cover and leave the chicken to braise on a low heat until cooked through and the gravy has thickened. If the gravy is not thick enough, stir in the cornflour slurry and cook until thick and glossy.

Remove the cloves of garlic and ginger slices, and serve warm with some steamed rice.

sunday
gatherings

Dinnertime was always the most important meal of the day for my family, because we'd sit down as a unit and discuss our day. Or, if we hadn't got much to say about that, we'd talk about the food we were eating, which my mum had prepared.

Now that my sisters and I have left home, this is a rarity. But when our schedules do coincide, it's usually on a Sunday that we enjoy a meal together. It's normally taken my mother a good few hours to prepare the food, and days beforehand she would have been asking us to make a decision on what we'd like to eat. We have lots of favourites, so is always a difficult choice to make!

In the morning, my mother starts the preparation, with pounding in the mortar and pestle or with the food processor getting a hammering. My dad then comes in and does the washing up, giving Mum a chance to have a cup of tea and a sit down. That's when I try to sneak a peek of what's to come. Soon she'll be shouting at my dad to get out of the kitchen, for taking too long or 'dilly dallying' as she says. She then proceeds to cook.

I used to wonder why she'd cook so much. I think it was so that there would be plenty for lunch the next day (most of this food tastes even better next day because the flavours have time to mature) but we have always been just too greedy and finished it all. Finally, once we are all well and truly stuffed, she'll collapse into a chair with great satisfaction.

"Chai Tow Kway"
Fried Carrot Cake

No, this recipe doesn't include carrots, or icing, cinnamon or sugar. We call mooli (white radish or daikon) 'white carrot' and it is this that we turn into a 'carrot cake', similar to the turnip cake dim sum. A lot of people are shocked when I say I make fried carrot cake at home, because it does require patience and a lot of time. Traditionally the mooli is shredded finely on a box grater, but these days a modern food processor with a shredder attachment does the job in seconds, saving the hard elbow grease.

You can prepare the carrot cake in advance, then have it ready for when you fancy surprising your guests with fried carrot cake. I love it in the morning as a nice alternative breakfast, garnished with some spicy chilli sambal. If you want to serve 4, use all of the radish cakes and double the remaining ingredients.

This version below is for the traditional white carrot cake. For the dark carrot cake, add 3 tablespoons of dark sweet soy sauce.

SERVES 1–2

For the radish cake (makes 2 portions)
100g fine rice flour (buy from an oriental supermarket)
150ml room-temperature water
150ml boiling water
200g mooli (white radish), peeled and finely shredded
¼ teaspoon sea salt

For the fried carrot cake
60g lard
4 garlic cloves, peeled and finely chopped
3 tablespoons *chai poh* (salted preserved radish), soaked in warm water for 5 minutes, drained and patted dry
1–2 tablespoons fish sauce (good-quality, such as Mega Chef, otherwise it can be too salty)
2 free-range eggs

Stir the rice flour and room-temperature water together in a heatproof bowl. Add the boiling water to the shredded mooli in another bowl, then pour the now-blanched mooli and water into the rice flour mixture. Add the salt. Set the bowl over a pan of boiling water to make a bain-marie and stir the mixture until it starts to thicken into a smooth sticky paste. Pour into a greased shallow heatproof dish (you want a layer of paste about 2cm thick). Place in a steamer and steam over medium-high heat for about 30 minutes or until cooked and kind of firm (it firms up more as it cools).

When completely cool, divide the radish cake in half and cut one half into little cubes. Don't worry about ragged edges as these are the bits that get irresistibly crispy (think roast potatoes). Keep the other half of the radish cake in an airtight container in the fridge for up to 5 days, or freeze it for use another day. (Defrost it thoroughly before use and then chop and use as below.)

Melt half the lard in a small frying pan or wok. When the lard is hot, add the cubes of radish cake and fry until crispy around the edges. I press on them with my spatula for maximum crispy edges. Add the rest of the lard to the pan, then fry the garlic and *chai poh* until fragrant. Add a drizzle of fish sauce. Spread everything out in the pan.

Beat the eggs with some fish sauce and pour evenly over the radish cake cubes. Leave to cook until set and the bottom is nicely browned, then flip over and brown on the other side. (To make this easier, just cut roughly into smaller portions with the sharp edge of your spatula before flipping, hawker-style. Hawkers can make servings of 20 carrot cakes at once, so an impressive single-move flip is not only idiotic but plain impossible. It's okay for everything to be semi-falling apart.)

Smear sambal over. (You can also fry the carrot cake directly with the sambal.) Finish with chopped spring onions and a little coriander and serve piping hot.

To finish
Sambal Tumis Belachan (see page 262) or Sambal Belachan (page 263)
chopped spring onions
coriander

In Singapore fish head is considered a delicacy, and a good head suitable for a claypot can cost more than the filleted fish itself. In the UK, as most fish heads are discarded, my mum would always baffle the fishmongers when she offered to pay for them. The fishmongers would often just give her the fish heads for free.

This dish is nourishing from the vegetables as well as the fish collagens and protein, and it is relatively cheap. It is a one-pot meal – my mum would cook it in a deep casserole and then just plonk the pot on the table. The only downside is that it is full of bones. If you are worried about this, you can substitute a salmon tail section. It will be just as effective.

Mix the marinade ingredients in a bowl, add the fish head and turn to coat. Set aside to marinate for 30 minutes. Drain, saving the marinade.

Heat 3 tablespoons of the oil in a flameproof casserole and add 2 slices of ginger and the fish head. Fry until the skin is golden brown. Be careful not to turn the fish head too much or it will break and fall apart. Set the fish head aside. Discard the oil.

Heat the casserole with the remaining oil, add the garlic and the rest of the ginger, and sauté until fragrant. Add the white part of the leek and fry for 30 seconds. Add the water and bring to the boil. Add the fish head and the reserved marinade. Add the Chinese cabbage, carrot, mushrooms and green part of the leek. Bring to a simmer, then cook for 30 minutes.

Taste and add a bit more salt if necessary, then carefully lower the tofu and vermicelli into the broth. Cover the casserole and cook gently for a minute or two.

To serve, add a dash of sesame oil and sprinkle with some white pepper before serving with steamed white rice.

SERVES 4–6

1 large or 2 small fish heads, about 750g
4 tablespoons cooking oil
4 thick slices of root ginger
1 garlic clove, smashed
1 leek, thickly sliced diagonally, green and white parts separated
1 litre water
5 leaves of Chinese cabbage, cut into 5cm slices
1 carrot, peeled and thinly sliced diagonally
4 pieces of dried shiitake mushroom, soaked until soft, drained and cut into bite-sized pieces
a 400g block firm tofu, cut into 8 cubes
250g dried rice vermicelli (*bee hoon*), soaked until soft and drained
toasted sesame oil
salt and white pepper

For the marinade
1 tablespoon light soy sauce
1 tablespoon rice wine (shaoxing or sake)
1 tablespoon fish sauce
½ teaspoon white pepper

"Nasi Goreng"
Indonesian Fried Rice

**Compared to the Chinese fried rice, this recipe is spicier, full
of shrimp and prawns and contains my favourite combination
of runny fried egg on top of rice. A perfect meal.**

SERVES 4

4 fresh, medium-hot, red Dutch
  chillies, roughly chopped,
  deseeded if preferred
1 garlic clove, peeled
1 banana shallot, peeled and
  roughly chopped
1 tablespoon toasted *belachan*
  (fermented shrimp paste)
4 tablespoons cooking oil
200g dried shrimps, soaked in hot
  water, drained and pounded fine
150g peeled raw prawns, deveined
2 tablespoons toasted sesame oil
600g cold cooked jasmine or
  long-grain rice
2 eggs, beaten
1 teaspoon salt, or to taste
1 teaspoon fish sauce, or to taste

Using a pestle and mortar, or a small food processor, pound/grind
the chillies with the garlic and shallot to make a paste, then mix in
the toasted *belachan*.

Heat the oil in a wok and fry the pounded dried shrimps until
fragrant. Add the chilli-garlic paste and cook for 5 minutes, stirring
constantly. Add the prawns and continue to stir for a few minutes
until they are cooked. Remove the sauce and prawns from the
wok and set aside.

Heat the sesame oil in the wok on a high heat. Add the cold rice
and stir well for 5 minutes to break it up. Make a well in the centre
of the rice and add the beaten eggs. Leave to cook until the egg
forms an omelette. Add the prawn-chilli mix and stir everything
together into the rice until thoroughly incorporated. Add the salt
and fish sauce to taste, then serve hot.

Variation:
Heat some cooking oil in the wok and fry the beaten eggs first.
Remove and set aside to cool, then cut up into strips. Continue
with the prawn-chilli mix and the rice. You have to use cold
cooked rice, otherwise the fried rice will just clump together
in one sticky mess. Add the omelette strips at the end.

This was a rarity in our house because my parents believed that the best Nasi Lemak, translated as 'fatty rice', came from a tiny little stall back home in Singapore, where you had to queue for at least 30 minutes to get breakfast. To me Nasi Lemak is the ultimate breakfast – fresh egg omelette (or hard-boiled eggs), fluffy coconut rice, rich and spicy sambal that slaps you around the face to wake up, and of course the *ikan bilis* (dried salted anchovies) and roasted peanut mix that I'd devour in 2 seconds. You can wrap it all up in a banana leaf but I find it much easier just serving on a sheet of banana leaf on a plate. This is my version, that finally, many years on, got my parents' stamp of approval.

First prepare the peanuts. Heat up 100ml rapeseed oil in a pan or wok to 120°C and slowly cook the peanuts for 25 minutes. Lift them out of the oil and drain on kitchen paper, then season with salt. Alternatively, roast the peanuts gently in the oven preheated to 160°C/140°C Fan/Gas Mark 3 for 10 minutes.

Heat up the peanut-frying oil to 170°C. Add the anchovies and fry until golden. Carefully lift the anchovies out of the oil and drain on kitchen paper; reserve the oil. Pat the anchovies dry and set aside until needed. (You can prepare the peanuts and anchovies in advance and keep in an airtight container for up to 5 days.)

Place the rice, coconut milk, water, pandan and garlic in a rice cooker and turn on to cook. Once the rice is ready, remove the garlic and pandan, then fluff up the rice and sprinkle the coconut cream powder liberally over the top. If you don't have the powder, spread the reserved coconut cream over the top and fluff after 5 minutes.

In a wok, heat up some of the peanut-frying oil (or fresh oil if you prefer) to fry the eggs. I love to have a runny yolk with my Nasi Lemak, so I fry the eggs sunny side up, carefully flicking the hot oil over them with a Chinese spatula to help cook the whites and make the egg go all crispy around the edges. Alternatively, you can whisk the eggs together and fry an omelette. Drain the fried eggs or omelette on kitchen paper.

Now you're ready to assemble the Nasi Lemak. Spoon the coconut rice into the middle of each bowl and garnish with the sliced cucumber, fried egg, anchovies, peanuts and a generous spoonful of sambal.

SERVES 4

For the coconut rice
240g Thai jasmine rice, rinsed well
125ml canned coconut milk (skim off the coconut cream from the top and reserve)
180ml water
3 pandan leaves, tied in a knot
1 garlic clove, peeled
2 tablespoons coconut cream powder

To serve
4 tablespoons peanuts (skin on)
about 100ml rapeseed oil
4 tablespoons dried salted anchovies (*ikan bilis*)
4 eggs
1 cucumber, thickly sliced
2 tablespoons Sambal Tumis Belachan (see page 262)
fine sea salt

"Pls Cian"
Fried Sea Bream with Thai Basil

This is my dad's favourite dish and Mum will cook this whenever
she can get hold of some Thai basil. Thai basil is super fragrant
with an almost aniseed flavour that pairs beautifully with fish
like sea bass or bream.

SERVES 4

1 whole sea bream or black bream,
   gutted and cleaned
4 tablespoons cooking oil
1 tablespoon cornflour
3 slices of root ginger, finely
   julienned
1 white or red onion, sliced
   medium fine
2 fresh, medium-hot, red Dutch
   chillies, deseeded and julienned,
   plus more to garnish
125g Thai basil, leaves and stalks
   roughly chopped
125g coriander, roughly chopped
3 spring onions, julienned, plus
   more to garnish

For the dressing
4 tablespoons lime or lemon juice
1 tablespoon soft brown sugar
2 teaspoons oyster sauce
2 tablespoons dark soy sauce
1 tablespoon light soy sauce
salt

Make 2 slashes on each side of the fish. Sprinkle salt on the fish
and rub well into the slashes. Pat dry and set aside.

Heat the oil in a non-stick pan or wok on a medium heat. Pat the
cornflour all over the fish, then add to the pan. Cook until golden
brown on the bottom, then turn the fish to cook on the other side.
Try not to move the fish too much as you don't want to break or
tear the skin. When both sides are golden brown, remove the fish
from the pan and set aside on a serving plate. Pour the oil into
a bowl and set aside. Quickly wash the pan.

Add 1 tablespoon of the oil from frying the fish to the clean pan.
Add the ginger, onion and chillies, and fry until fragrant. Add the
dressing ingredients and stir until the sugar has dissolved. Taste
to check the flavour: add a little extra sugar if too sour or an extra
squeeze of lime or lemon juice if too sweet.

Add the Thai basil, coriander and spring onions. Mix well with
the sauce, then pour on top of the fish. Garnish with some extra
julienned chilli and spring onions. Serve with fresh steamed rice.

Hainanese Chicken Rice

I remember watching my mum making this dish. My version here is how my mum would cook it. It's really difficult because there's no defined rule about how to make it, but is all about tasting and using your senses to suit your preferences. Its success depends on the ingredients you use and the time and effort you put in to make it right. You certainly can't rush it and you need to take care with all of the components – some would say that the rice is more important than the poached chicken. My favourite memory of this dish is my mum Asian-squatting on the newspaper-covered floor and using her scarily intimidating cleaver to smash down through the chicken bones with surgical precision. I don't recommend doing this unless you are happy to have chicken bones in your food – I joint the chicken to serve. Be sure to use a good-quality, free-range bird no bigger than 1.2kg as otherwise it would take too long to poach. If cooking for more people, I recommend using two smaller birds rather than one larger one, as this gives a better flavour to the stock.

Many people don't realise that chicken fat is key to this dish. Ask your butcher for chicken skin or fat, which they normally would give you free. Failing that, the inner cavity of supermarket chickens normally has fat pockets that you can just tear out.

SERVES 4–6

3–4 litres water, depending on the size of the chicken
a thumb-sized piece of root ginger, peeled and thickly sliced
3–4 pandan leaves, tied into a knot
a 1–1.2kg chicken, inside fat removed and reserved
8 garlic cloves, smashed
toasted sesame oil for coating
fine sea salt

For the rice
2 tablespoons rendered chicken fat (see method), or cooking oil
8 garlic cloves, peeled and crushed
a thumb-sized piece of root ginger, peeled and thickly sliced
480g Thai jasmine rice, rinsed
3–4 pandan leaves, tied into a knot
a pinch of fine sea salt (optional)

Use a large stockpot that is taller than it is wide, as you want the chicken to be just covered with enough water to poach it. Heat the water in the pot. Add trimmings from the ginger and the pandan leaves to flavour the stock as well as the green parts of the spring onions for garnish.

Rub the chicken generously with fine sea salt all over the skin and inside the cavity, then rinse off with cold water. This gives you a much smoother skin finish, so don't skip this step (be careful when rinsing not to splash all around the kitchen, and make sure to wash your hands after handling the chicken). Stuff the chicken with the garlic, ginger and pandan leaves. Set aside ready to poach.

Put any chicken fat and/or skin you have gathered into a saucepan and render the fat on a medium heat. Set the rendered fat aside.

When the water in the stockpot comes to the boil, it's ready for the chicken. Hold it over the pot and either dunk the chicken into the water to fill the cavity, then lift it out, or ladle the hot water into the cavity of the chicken. The objective is to help warm the chicken through for a more even poach. Place the chicken back in the water and turn the heat down to a very gentle simmer. Cover and poach for about 30 minutes.

Check to see if the chicken is cooked – the meatiest part behind the thigh should register 73°C on a probe thermometer. If it doesn't, remove the pot from the heat and leave the chicken to cook in the residual heat of the water for a further 20 minutes or until it reaches temperature. Cooking time will depend on the size of the bird.

Lift the chicken out of the stock and place immediately in an ice-bath that's seasoned with fine sea salt. Cool for 15 minutes to prevent the chicken from overcooking and to ensure that prized glutinous skin. (If you would prefer to have warm meat, omit the ice-bath.) Transfer the chicken to a tray and pat dry, then coat with toasted sesame oil. Leave to rest for at least 15 minutes (total resting time from cooking is around 30 minutes if you have skipped the ice-bath stage).

While the chicken is resting, taste the chicken stock and season with salt if necessary, then use some of the stock to cook the rice. Heat up a wok with the rendered chicken fat (or cooking oil), add the garlic and ginger, and sauté for 3–4 minutes to release the fragrance. Add the rice and stir in quickly to coat each grain with the rendered fat, garlic and ginger. Transfer the rice mixture to the rice cooker. Add 550ml of the chicken stock, the pandan leaves and salt (if needed). Turn on the rice cooker to cook.

Reduce the remaining stock to about 2 litres, season with the pepper and keep hot.

While the stock is reducing, prep the sauces to go with the chicken rice, the dressing and the garnishes. Put all the ingredients for the chilli sauce into a blender and blend until smooth. (How much chilli you use depends on how spicy you want the sauce to be; for a less spicy sauce, add more lime juice

For the soup
reserved reduced chicken stock (see method)
½ teaspoon white pepper
watercress or thinly sliced Chinese leaves (optional)

For the chilli sauce
10–12 (180g) fresh, medium-hot, red Dutch chillies, deseeded and chopped
5–6 (8g) bird's eye chillies (optional)
3 garlic cloves, peeled
5 slices (12g) of root ginger, peeled
2 tablespoons caster sugar
4 tablespoons white rice vinegar
1 tablespoon chicken stock
1 teaspoon sea salt
lime juice to taste

For the garlic and ginger sauce
5 garlic cloves, peeled and blanched
a slice of root ginger, peeled
50ml hot reserved reduced chicken stock (see method)
1 tablespoon caster sugar
1 teaspoon salt

For the dressing
2 tablespoons rice wine (shaoxing or sake)
2 tablespoons soy sauce
2 tablespoons toasted sesame oil

...Continued on page 199

and stock.) Pour into a bowl. Put the ingredients for the garlic and ginger sauce into the cleaned blender and blend until smooth. For the dressing, mix together the rice wine, soy sauce and sesame oil in a small bowl.

Portion the chicken into thighs and drumsticks, wings and breasts. Separate the chicken fillet from each breast, then give the breast a little squash and slice it.

Serve the chicken on a platter with the cucumber underneath – my mum would always place breast (white) meat on one side for my husband and herself, and leg or thigh (dark meat) on the other side for the rest of us. Ladle a little hot reduced stock over the top, followed by the dressing, then garnish with coriander and spring onions. Strain the remaining reduced stock and serve in bowls with the watercress or Chinese leaf, if using, and the sauces on the side with sweet soy sauce.

Tip: If I run out of time to prep the 2 accompanying sauces, I don't see any shame in using shop bought sriracha chilli sauce (Flying Goose brand), mixed with a little sugar, lime juice and chicken stock. Please don't tell my mum though.

To serve
**1 cucumber, peeled and
thickly sliced
small bunch of coriander,
leaves picked
2 spring onions (white parts),
julienned (reserve the green
tops for the stock)**
kecap manis **(sweet soy sauce)
for dipping (optional)**

Smoked Ox Cheek Rendang

If making the Beef Rendang on page 203 means that someone loves you, this one means they'll love you for life! It's a dish that I created when I was working at the Smokehouse in Islington, a heady combination of tradition and flavours that work perfectly together. The method is pretty much the same as for Beef Rendang; however, you hot-smoke the meat beforehand. Don't be put off by the addition of bone marrow, as it mostly melts into the dish to keep it succulent!

SERVES 4

1kg ox cheeks, trimmed
(ask your butcher to
remove any tight sinew)
sea salt
1kg bone marrow
4 tablespoons desiccated coconut
3 tablespoons cooking oil
2 cinnamon sticks
1 tablespoon ground coriander
1 teaspoon ground cumin
5 kaffir lime leaves
a 240ml can coconut milk
2 teaspoons salt
1 tablespoon dark soy sauce

For the rempah
a 5cm piece of fresh galangal,
peeled and roughly chopped
a 2.5cm piece of root ginger, peeled
and roughly chopped
2 lemongrass stalks, woody ends
removed and stalks roughly
chopped
2 small red onions, cut into large
chunks
3 garlic cloves, peeled
3–6 fresh, medium-hot, red
Dutch chillies (depending
on personal taste)
2 tablespoons water

Prepare a hot smoker or barbecue. Cover the ox cheeks with sea salt to season (don't use pepper here as it can burn and add bitterness), then hot-smoke for at least 4 hours (depending on size) or until they reach an internal temperature of 93°C (check with a probe thermometer). For the last hour, add the bone marrow to smoke with the cheeks. You're aiming for the marrow to go from hard to soft. Use tongs to remove the meat from the smoker. Gently scoop the marrow out of the bone and set aside. Wrap the ox cheeks in baking parchment or butcher's paper to keep it from drying out.

Heat a non-stick frying pan on a low heat and add the desiccated coconut. Dry-fry the coconut, constantly moving it around in the pan, until golden brown. Cool, then grind in a blender to a smooth paste. Tip into a small bowl.

Grind the ingredients for the *rempah* in the cleaned blender (adding them in the order listed) to make a smooth paste.

Heat the oil in a heavy-based flameproof casserole and add the *rempah* and cinnamon sticks. Fry, stirring constantly, on a low heat for about 5 minutes or until fragrant.

Preheat the oven to 140°C/120°C Fan/Gas Mark 1.

Dice the ox cheeks, then add to the casserole and fry until well coated with the paste. When the meat is coated, add the coriander, cumin, desiccated coconut paste and lime leaves. Stir until well mixed, then add the coconut milk followed by the salt and soy sauce. Stir. Bring to the boil, then lower the heat, cover the pot and simmer for 20 minutes.

Transfer the casserole to the oven and leave to braise for 4–5 hours. Give the mixture a stir after 2–2½ hours, then add the bone marrow pieces. Return to the oven to finish cooking, uncovered to help the rendang dry out more. (You can also use a slow cooker.) When ready, give the rendang a good stir and serve with plain steamed rice.

A special dish in our family, here beef is slowly braised to get it to that falling-apart stage with huge rich flavour. Because it takes hours, my mum has always said: 'If someone made this from scratch for you, that means they truly love you!' Like most curries, this develops even more flavour if you cook it the day before serving. You can also add 500g peeled potatoes, cut into large chunks, with the coconut milk, to bulk out the dish more.

SERVES 4

4 tablespoons desiccated coconut
3 tablespoons cooking oil
2 cinnamon sticks
1kg boneless beef shin or ox cheek,
    cut into 5cm cubes
1 tablespoon ground coriander
1 teaspoon ground cumin
5 kaffir lime leaves
a 240ml can coconut milk
2 teaspoons salt
1 tablespoon dark soy sauce

For the rempah
a 5cm piece of fresh galangal,
    peeled and roughly chopped
a 2.5cm piece of root ginger, peeled
    and roughly chopped
2 lemongrass stalks, wood ends
    removed and stalks roughly
    chopped
2 small red onions, cut into
    large chunks
3 garlic cloves, peeled
3–6 fresh, medium-hot, red
    Dutch chillies (depending
    on personal taste)
2 tablespoons water

Heat a non-stick frying pan on a low heat and add the desiccated coconut. Dry-fry the coconut, constantly moving it around in the pan, until golden brown. Cool, then grind in a blender to a smooth paste. Tip into a small bowl.

Grind the ingredients for the *rempah* in the cleaned blender, adding them in the order listed, to make a smooth paste. Add a splash of water if necessary.

Heat the oil in a heavy-based flameproof casserole and add the *rempah* and cinnamon sticks. Fry, constantly stirring, on a low heat for about 5 minutes or until fragrant.

Preheat the oven to 140°C/120°C Fan/Gas Mark 1.

Add the beef to the casserole and fry until browned all over and well coated with the spice paste. Add the coriander, cumin, desiccated coconut paste and lime leaves. Stir until well mixed, then add the coconut milk followed by the salt and soy sauce. Stir. Bring to the boil, then lower the heat, cover the pot and simmer for 20 minutes.

Transfer the casserole to the oven and leave to braise for 4–5 hours or until the beef is really tender. Give the mixture a stir every now and then, and you should be left with a rather dry, braised curry with not much liquid other than the oils from the coconut and meat. (You can also use a slow cooker.)

When ready, give the rendang a good stir and serve with plain steamed rice.

Crisp Roast Pork Belly

You'll need a bit of patience with this recipe as you can't rush the marinading of the pork, and it needs a little bit of time in the oven to get the best, crispiest skin.

Make sure you buy a piece of pork belly that has a good layer of fat and meat in it. The belly should be 3–3.5cm thick at least.

SERVES 6

1kg pork belly
2 tablespoons rice wine (shaoxing
   or sake) or vodka
2 tablespoons sea salt

For the marinade
2 garlic cloves, finely crushed
2 teaspoons finely chopped
   root ginger
2 teaspoons salt
1 teaspoon five-spice powder
½ teaspoon white pepper

Rinse the pork belly and pat dry with kitchen paper. Use a skewer or the end of a sharp knife to prick the skin all over, then rub the skin with the wine. Score vertically the inner portion of the meat. Do not score the skin.

Combine the marinade ingredients in a bowl. Rub evenly over the meat, particularly into the scored underside. Do not rub the marinade on the skin. You want to keep this dry. Place the pork on a tray, skin side up. Leave to marinate, uncovered, in the fridge for 2–6 hours to dry out the skin.

Preheat the oven to 230°C/210°C Fan/Gas Mark 8.

Fill a roasting tin with water, around 2cm deep, then place a roasting rack in the pan. Place the pork belly on the rack, skin side up. Spread the salt over the skin. Roast for 20 minutes or until a white salt layer has formed on the skin.

Remove the meat from the oven. Using a small knife, gently scrape off the white salt layer from the skin. Put the meat back on the roasting rack and roast for a further 20–25 minutes or until the bubbles that form on the skin pop. The skin should be golden brown at this stage.

Remove from the oven and leave the pork belly to rest for 15–20 minutes before cutting it up into serving portions of 3cm-thick slices. It will be easiest to cut the pork by placing it skin side down and using a heavy cleaver or knife.

celebration meals

These are our favourite dishes when we come together to celebrate an occasion or just to celebrate. My parents used to hold lots of parties for family and friends at our home. Mum would normally cook a giant hot pot and prep a million raw ingredients like chicken, mackerel, pork, vegetables, squid, you name it – it all went into a hot pot. There'd be a loud clashing sound from a mahjong table going in the corner, with the occasional 'GAME!' being shouted across the room. The youngest children would be running around the house and playing. And I'd be hovering around the kitchen, getting in the way, but trying to see if there was anything to nibble on.

As we got older, the parties were less frequent because it was harder to get our friends and family together regularly. This is a shame because we had felt we were part of a community. Now everyone has grown up or moved away and lost touch, so if there's an occasion or excuse to celebrate, we make a big deal of it and prepare one of these dishes. The recipes take time and patience but are well worth the effort. They also take plenty of time to eat, so there is space to talk, to celebrate and enjoy.

Fresh live brown crab tended to be on the expensive side, so this was always a special treat meal at home. My dad and I would fight over the crab and could easily go through 2 crabs each, creating piles of crab shells and debris. When I cook crab, I always save the shells and simmer them with ginger and garlic to make a tasty crab stock for my congee or other dishes.

Wash the crab well under cold running water, using a clean brush and sponge to ensure it is completely clean. Remove the gills and spilt the crab into quarters. Crack the claws and body to help them cook evenly.

Put the pieces of crab into a deep heatproof dish that fits inside a steamer. Add the spring onions, ginger, salt, vermouth and rice wine. Steam on a high heat for 10 minutes; it is cooked when the shell and the meat turn a red-orange colour.

Carefully remove the dish from the steamer. Garnish with more spring onions and ginger and the chillies, and serve steaming hot.

SERVES 4

a 1–1.2kg brown crab

4 spring onions (white parts), thinly sliced, plus more to garnish

a 4cm piece of root ginger, peeled and thinly sliced, plus more to garnish

1 teaspoon salt

1 tablespoon dry vermouth

1 tablespoon rice wine (shaoxing or sake)

2 fresh, medium-hot, red Dutch chillies, deseeded and thinly sliced

Singapore Chilli Crab

Despite its name, Singapore chilli crab isn't particularly spicy. Its sauce has a delicious delicate balance between salty, sweet and heat from the chilli.

You really need to use clean crabs, so don't skip the washing. You could also ask your fishmonger to do this for you.

SERVES 4

a 1–1.2kg brown crab
6 fresh, medium-hot, red Dutch
  chillies
a 1cm piece of root ginger, peeled
  and roughly chopped
2 banana shallots, peeled
8 garlic cloves, peeled
2 tablespoons cooking oil
1 tablespoon fermented
  soya-bean paste
300ml Chicken Stock
  (see page 279) or water
2 tablespoons caster sugar
1 teaspoon toasted sesame oil
4 tablespoons tomato ketchup
1 teaspoon hot chilli powder
  (optional)
1 tablespoon cornflour
2 tablespoons water
2 eggs, beaten
salt and white pepper
2 spring onions (white parts),
  thinly sliced, to garnish

Wash the crab well under cold running water, using a clean brush and sponge to ensure it is spotlessly clean. Remove the gills and spilt the crab into quarters. Crack the claws and body to help them cook evenly. Set aside.

Grind the chillies, ginger, shallots and garlic together in a blender to make a paste. Heat the oil in a wok or large sauté pan on a medium heat and cook the paste for a couple of minutes, stirring constantly. Add the crab to the pan and mix well with the paste.

Stir in the fermented soya-bean paste and cook for 3 minutes, then add the stock or water and bring to the boil. Mix in the sugar, sesame oil, tomato ketchup and 1 teaspoon salt. Once the sauce comes back to the boil, stir in the chilli powder, if using. Cover with a lid and turn down to a simmer, then cook for 3 more minutes. Check that the crab is cooked by noticing the change of colour in the shell, and if the meat is transparent, cook for a bit longer.

Whisk the cornflour, water and beaten eggs together. Add to the pan and stir for about 1 minute or until the sauce thickens. Season with salt and white pepper.

Garnish with spring onions and serve immediately with plenty of napkins. Take care when eating the sauce as it may have shards of crab shell and cartilage in it.

Steamed Mussels with Pancetta and Miso

As a family we used to travel to France a lot, and my favourite thing to eat there would be a bucket of *moules marinières* with a large baguette to dip into the sauce. I remember my dad saying how proud of us he was when Frenchmen were shocked to see 2 small girls finishing nearly a kilo of mussels without a fuss. This is my version that I like to cook at home.

Heat up the oil in a large saucepan (with a lid) and sauté the garlic, pancetta and shallots for a couple of minutes. Turn the heat up, and after a minute or two add the mussels and give them a good stir. Add the rice wine to the pan, cover with a lid and steam for 5 minutes. Give the pan a little shake every now and then to help open the mussels.

When all the mussels have opened up, lift them out of the liquid and place in a serving bowl. Discard any mussels that haven't opened.

Stir the miso and butter into the cooking liquid and boil down to reduce by half, then add the chopped parsley and black pepper. Pour over the mussels and serve.

SERVES 4

2 tablespoons cooking oil
2 garlic cloves, thinly sliced
250g pancetta, diced, or diced
    streaky bacon
2 banana shallots, thinly sliced
1kg mussels, cleaned and scrubbed
250ml rice wine (shaoxing or sake)
    or dry white wine
1 teaspoon sweet white miso paste
50g unsalted butter, cubed

To garnish
chopped parsley
cracked black pepper

Singapore Laksa

You can be as creative as you want with this dish – add chicken, squid or even mussels. A few tablespoons of brown crab meat stirred into the prawn stock will enrich it nicely. Chinese fish cakes and laksa leaves can be found at good Oriental/Asian shops. If you can't find laksa leaves, you can use coriander leaves instead.

SERVES 4

For the rempah
5 candlenuts or macadamia nuts
a 2cm piece of fresh galangal, peeled
125g banana shallots, peeled and roughly chopped
4–5 fresh, medium-hot, red Dutch chillies, deseeded, peeled and chopped
2 tablespoons dried shrimps, soaked in boiling water for 20 minutes, drained and patted dry
½ teaspoon ground turmeric
½ tablespoon *belachan* (fermented shrimp paste), toasted

For the laksa
a 400ml can coconut milk
250g dried rice vermicelli
750ml water
250g large raw prawns (shell on)
2 tablespoons cooking oil
1 lemongrass stalk, crushed
½ tablespoon ground coriander
1–2 teaspoons salt
1 teaspoon caster sugar
150g beansprouts, topped and tailed, blanched in boiling water for 30 seconds and drained
1–2 fried Chinese fish cakes, sliced 5mm thick
1 cucumber, peeled and cut into thin curls on a spiraliser or into strips
4 hard boiled eggs, halved
a small bunch of laksa leaves, shredded

Grind all the *rempah* ingredients together in a blender (adding them in the order listed) until smooth, thinning with 2–3 tablespoons of the coconut milk from the laksa ingredients. Keep to one side.

Soak the rice vermicelli in warm water for 30 minutes, then drain.

Meanwhile, bring the water to the boil in a medium saucepan. Add the prawns and blanch for about 2 minutes or until they turn pink. Lift the prawns out of the stock. Reserve the pan of stock.

Peel the prawns and set aside. Throw the heads and shells back into the pan of stock. Bring to the boil and simmer for 15 minutes. Strain the stock and discard the prawn shells.

Heat the oil in a large saucepan, add the *rempah* and cook, stirring, for 2–3 minutes or until fragrant. Add the lemongrass and cook over a low heat for 10 minutes, stirring often to prevent the paste from sticking to the bottom of the pan. Add a splash of water occasionally to stop it burning. Stir in the ground coriander and cook for a further 5 minutes (adding more water as needed).

Pour in the prawn stock, stir and simmer for about 5 minutes. Add the rest of the coconut milk and stir until the soup boils, then lower the heat and simmer for 10–15 minutes. Season with salt and add the sugar to give the soup a rounder flavour. Remove the crushed lemongrass stalks and discard.

Bring a pot of water to the boil. Add the softened rice vermicelli and blanch them for a second. It is important not to overcook. Drain. (If using thicker noodles for laksa, you'll need to boil them longer until they are cooked.)

To serve, divide the prawns and all the remaining ingredients, except the laksa leaves, among 4 bowls. Ladle the soup into the bowls and scatter the shredded laksa leaves on top.

"Lor Arkh"
Teochew Soy-braised Duck

There are several great hawkers in Singapore that do a perfect Teochew-style soy-braised duck but none are better than my mum's. Duck dishes were always a special treat in our household, because duck was quite expensive when I was growing up. So we appreciated every single bit of it, including the liver and heart. The recipe may look long but it's totally worth the extra effort. More eggs and tofu can be added to serve more people. You can also add more or less honey, salt, soy sauce and pepper. It's all up to your own taste preferences.

SERVES 4–6

1 duck, around 2–2.5kg, with the
  duck liver
1 tablespoon salt (to rub over
  the duck)
5 hard-boiled eggs, peeled
250g firm tofu

For the marinade
1½ teaspoons five-spice powder
½ teaspoon salt
½ tablespoon dark soy sauce
  (preferably thick)

For the braising liquid
1 tablespoon cooking oil
2 star anise
20 garlic cloves, peeled
150g fresh galangal, peeled and
  thickly sliced
120g root ginger, peeled and
  thinly sliced
100g palm sugar, shaved or
  crumbled
2 litres water
1 teaspoon toasted sesame oil
1¼ tablespoons honey
2½ tablespoons rice wine
  (shaoxing or sake)

Rub the duck all over with salt, including inside the cavity, then rinse thoroughly. Dry the duck by patting with kitchen paper.

For the marinade, rub the five-spice powder all over the duck, inside and out. Put the salt into the cavity and rub it in. Rub the dark soy sauce all over the duck skin. Set the duck aside to come to room temperature.

Meanwhile, make the braising liquid. Add the cooking oil to a hot wok on a high heat. Add the star anise, garlic, galangal and ginger. Stir-fry for a couple of minutes until fragrant, then add the palm sugar and continue to fry for about 2 minutes.

Transfer the spice mixture to a large pot that is big enough to hold the duck. Add the water and stir, then add the remaining ingredients for the braising liquid. Bring to the boil and boil for a few minutes to season the water.

Carefully lower the duck and liver into the liquid, making sure that there's liquid in the cavity of the duck as this will help poach it evenly. Cook for 3 minutes, breast side up, then lower the heat to a simmer.

After 10 minutes of simmering, carefully prick the duck several times all over with a fork to release the fat from under the skin. Carefully turn the duck over using tongs and continue to braise gently on a simmer for 30 minutes. This will ensure it cooks evenly and gets a lovely even colour.

After 30 minutes, remove the liver from the pan – it should be firm but soft enough when poked with a fork. Set aside.

Continue simmering the duck for 15 minutes, then remove the star anise (unless you want a stronger anise flavour). After a further 5 minutes of simmering, add the hard-boiled eggs to the pan to braise and absorb the colour and flavour of the stock. Turn the duck over again.

Simmer for a further 40 minutes (a total cooking time of 1½ hours). The duck should be tender and the eggs evenly coloured. Remove the eggs and duck carefully from the braising liquid using a large strainer.

Add the firm tofu to the braising liquid to cook for 10 minutes on a simmer. Remove the tofu, galangal and garlic with a slotted spoon or tongs. Using a large spoon, skim off the layer of oil that has formed on the top of the braising liquid. If you want a thicker gravy, slowly add cornflour slurry, whisking to ensure there are no lumps.

Chop up the duck and halve the eggs. Place on a serving platter along with the duck liver and sliced braised tofu. Drizzle gravy generously over the top. Garnish with coriander and slices of cucumber.

2¼ tablespoons mushroom-flavoured superior dark soy sauce
2¼ tablespoons dark soy sauce (preferably thick)
3 tablespoons oyster sauce
½ teaspoon salt

For the slurry (optional)
1 tablespoon cornflour
1 tablespoon water

To garnish
coriander sprigs
sliced peeled cucumber

Anyone who knows me, knows how much I adore Parisian bistro food and in particular beef tartare. It's something about the texture of the beef mixed with the sharp sauce that brings me so much joy. My version is just as sharp but mixed with a bit more spice and heat. I like to use a cut like beef rump instead of the traditional fillet because I love the texture and flavour of the meat. If you can get hold of Dexter beef rump, that would be perfect for this dish.

For the pickled shallots, bring the red wine vinegar, sugar, water and salt to the boil in a small saucepan. Pour over the shallot rings in a bowl and set aside to pickle for 5 minutes, then drain and discard the pickle liquid.

Mix the sauce ingredients together in a bowl. Adjust the seasoning with more salt and soy sauce, or with a little sugar if you want it sweeter. Slice the beef thinly, then dice the slices into roughly 3mm pieces. Add to the sauce along with the toasted hazelnuts and sesame seeds. Give it a really good stir.

Serve the tartare with toasted sourdough, pickled shallots and a sprinkle of Parmesan on top for extra umami.

SERVES 4

400g well-aged boneless beef rump, fat removed and trimmed
50g hazelnuts, toasted and roughly chopped
1 tablespoon white sesame seeds, toasted

For the pickled shallots
50ml red wine vinegar
50g caster sugar
50ml water
a pinch of salt
1 large banana shallot, thinly sliced into rings

For the sauce
½ tablespoon Gochujang paste (red chilli paste)
2 tablespoons toasted sesame oil
1 teaspoon soy sauce
2 teaspoons Chinese black vinegar
½ teaspoon Dijon mustard
1 teaspoon Tabasco sauce
caster sugar (optional)
salt

To serve
toasted sourdough bread
grated Parmesan
4 egg yolks

sweets

From drinks to desserts, these sweet recipes are the best way to end a meal. Nonya desserts are particularly sweet, but also focus on texture by using ingredients like agar or tapioca. One dessert in particular stands out to me. This is the Chendol on page 257, which is like a pick and mix of different ingredients and textures and is completely satisfying after a big heavy meal. I remember taking my husband, Steele, to Old Airport Road Market in Singapore to have his first Chendol. He was speechless. The texture of the cold, sweet coconut milk, ice shavings, rich coffee flavour from the palm sugar and clean sweetness from the pandan meant that he didn't share any with us and bought a second one before he had finished his first.

Some of the desserts in this chapter are simpler and lighter on the tummy. The Sweet Potatoes in Ginger Syrup on page 239 was a particular favourite of mine while I was pregnant with Riley – the ginger syrup was very good at calming my queasy stomach.

I've also included my favourite drinks, the ones I immediately buy when I'm back in Singapore. They all go so well with the recipes in this book. For example, when I can get hold of calamansi, I make Lime Juice (see page 228) to serve with some of the spicier dishes like laksa because it has a cooling effect to balance the chilli.

Lime Juice

In Singapore calamansi limes are very common but it's really hard to get hold of them elsewhere because once they are picked, they degrade really quickly. The calamansi is a hybrid between orange and lime – it has orange pulp with sour, tart juice. I think that calamansi lime imparts greater flavour than Japanese yuzu, and unlike other varieties of lime it has an intense citrusy fragrance. You can of course make this juice using the limes widely available in Britain.

SERVES 1

5 calamansi (or regular limes),
 cut in half
2 tablespoons caster sugar
250ml water
a handful of ice
50ml soda water

Squeeze the juice from the limes. Pour into a glass, add the sugar and water, and stir well. Finish with ice and soda water.

Home-made Soy Milk

I love a glass of fresh soy milk in the morning, to combat the heat in Singapore, but also equally enjoy a warm, sweet glass of this at home in the UK. When I was trying to get Riley to try different milks other than cow's milk, he took to this immediately because it can be as sweet or natural as you want. You'll need a high-powered blender, to extract as much 'milk' as possible from the beans. The milk will keep for up to 3 days refrigerated. You will need a large stock pot for this, though this recipe halves easily if you want to make less. My family would finish this in seconds!

Rinse the soya beans thoroughly, then soak them overnight in water to cover. The next day, drain well, discarding the water, and rinse the soya beans a few times. Remove the soya bean skins as much as you can. Drain well again.

Working in batches, blitz the soya beans in a blender until smooth, adding some of the measured water as needed. Transfer the blended soya beans and remaining water to a big non-stick pot.

Bring the soya bean mixture to the boil on a medium heat. Stir occasionally to prevent the beans from sticking to the bottom of the pot, skimming any foam that rises to the top. As soon as the mixture boils, lower the heat to medium-low and simmer for 30–45 minutes or until the soy milk has reduced to your desired consistency (I like my soy milk thicker so I boil it longer).

Remove from the heat and pour the soy milk through a muslin-lined sieve, or a paper or cloth coffee filter, into a bowl to strain out the soya bean residue. Let the soy milk cool down then squeeze the residue to make sure that all soy milk is fully extracted. Discard the residue.

Add sugar syrup to taste before serving the soy milk. I find if you have this iced or served cold, you'll require a touch more sugar.

MAKES 2–3 LITRES, ACCORDING TO THICKNESS

680g organic, non-GMO dried
  soya beans
6.5 litres water
Sugar Syrup (see page 266), to taste

Milo Dinosaur

Milo is a chocolate malt drink, but also marketed as an energy drink (I think that's because it tends to be so sweet). It is sold in many countries and is a firm favourite for those who know of it. Riley goes nuts for Milo, particularly this Milo Dinosaur. In Singapore, this and Godzilla (below) are the most popular drinks for the young ones.

SERVES 1

7 tablespoons Milo powder
½ tablespoon sweetened
   condensed milk
crushed ice

Mix 5 tablespoons of the Milo powder with the condensed milk in a huge heatproof glass. Fill the glass halfway with hot water and stir well to mix and dissolve the Milo. Add enough crushed ice to fill the glass, then spoon the rest of the Milo powder on top. Serve with a straw.

Variation: Milo Godzilla
Top the Milo Dinosaur with a scoop of ice cream (see page 250) or whipped cream. I love to add a touch of Kaya (page 249) to make this more like a Milo sundae if I'm spoiling the family.

This is a perfect dessert for the summer, or if you've had too much spicy food and need cooling down. My little trick is to drain the syrup from the lychees and freeze it in an ice-cube tray, then serve a couple of lychee ice cubes in the bowls for an extra cooling effect. This jelly is a firm set.

Soak the agar strips in a bowl of cold water for 5 minutes.

Pour the 2.5 litres water into a large pot and bring to the boil. Drain the agar strips using a strainer and add to the boiling water, or whisk in the agar powder if using. Stir occasionally to dissolve the strips. Add the gelatine powder solution and the sugar and turn the heat down to low. Continue to stir to dissolve any lumps, then remove from the heat.

When the jelly mixture starts to thicken, strain it through a fine sieve into a bowl. Press down on the mixture in the sieve to extract as much liquid as possible, then add the evaporated milk and almond extract and stir well. Set aside to cool.

Pour the jelly mixture into 2 large bowls or deep trays. Cool for about 30 minutes at room temperature, then chill in the fridge for 4 hours or overnight until the jelly sets. Pour the lychees and their syrup into a bowl and chill as well (unless you are making syrup ice cubes).

When ready to serve, spoon the almond jelly into dessert bowls. Top each with lychees and drizzle some of the lychee syrup over.

SERVES 12

30g agar strips, cut into 2.5cm pieces (or the same amount of agar powder)
2.5 litres water
1½ teaspoons gelatine powder, dissolved in 200ml water
600g caster sugar
375ml evaporated milk
1 tablespoon almond extract
2 x 565g cans lychees in syrup

Coconut Sago with Palm Sugar Syrup

Whenever I'm standing outside a sweets stall in a hawker in Singapore, my eyes always make a greedy beeline for coconut sago. I find the mixture of the salty coconut with the sweet, toffee-like flavours of *gula melaka* (palm sugar syrup) so satisfying, especially in the 35°C sweltering heat.

SERVES 4

250g sago or tapioca pearls
4 pandan leaves, tied into a knot
300ml canned coconut milk
1 quantity Palm Sugar Syrup
    (see page 266)
salt

Rinse the sago or tapioca pearls, then soak them in cold water for at least an hour. Rinse and drain again after the soaking. Transfer the pearls and pandan leaves to a pot and cover with enough water so that the water level is at least 4cm above the pearls.

Bring the water to the boil, stirring constantly so that the pearls don't stick to the bottom of the pan. Stir for 5–10 minutes or until the pearls turn translucent, then remove immediately from the heat and drain in a sieve. Rinse the pearls under cold running water, using a spoon to keep the pearls moving and prevent them from clumping together.

Divide the pearls among small 4 serving bowls. Leave in the fridge to chill for 2–3 hours.

Warm the coconut milk with 1½ teaspoons salt.

To serve, turn out the sago or tapioca pearls (or keep in the bowls). Generously drizzle palm sugar syrup and warmed coconut milk over the top.

Sweet Potatoes in Ginger Syrup

Ginger is thought to have healing properties – *pukol angin* (to beat the toxic gases and dampness out of you to relieve aches and pains). This is why postnatal mothers were given lots of ginger to 'beat the wind'. It's not common here to have sweet potato as a dessert, but I really enjoy this soothing combination. The strongest ginger is just beneath the skin, so to get the most flavour out of it don't peel it.

Scrub the sweet potatoes (don't peel), then cut into 5cm chunks. Put them into a heatproof bowl, set in a steamer and steam for 15–30 minutes or until softened.

Meanwhile, put the sugar and water into a large saucepan and stir to dissolve. Add the ginger and bring to the boil. Boil for a few minutes, then remove from the heat and set aside.

Remove the sweet potatoes from the steamer and cool, then peel off the skin. Transfer to the pan of ginger syrup and leave to steep for at least an hour. Serve warm.

SERVES 6–8

900g sweet potatoes
250g caster sugar
1.5 litres water
2 knobs of root ginger, sliced
 into 5mm-thick pieces

"Bubur Pulot Hitam"
Black Glutinous Rice Porridge
with Coconut

Although *pulot hitam* literally translates as black glutinous rice, this rice pudding is more of a purplish colour. It has long been my favourite dessert, and I would always request extra thick coconut milk on top because I love the sweet and saltiness of it. This works incredibly well with a big scoop of Coconut Ice Cream (see page 250), playing on the senses with hot, cold, sweet and salty. It's best to make this dessert in a deep pot, to prevent the liquid from evaporating too quickly and becoming dry. And don't rush the soaking of the rice – it needs a decent amount of soaking time to help open up the grains, otherwise it will take forever to cook.

SERVES 4

230g black glutinous rice
2.5 litres water
6 pandan leaves, tied in a knot
175ml thick canned coconut milk
   (shake the can to mix
   the contents)
230g palm sugar, scraped into
   fragments or grated
2 tablespoons caster sugar
¼ teaspoon salt
1 quantity Palm Sugar Syrup
   (see page 266)

Put the rice into a bowl and cover with enough water to come at least 2.5cm above the rice. Leave to soak overnight to soften the rice.

Drain the rice and put it into a large saucepan with the 2.5 litres of water, the pandan leaves and 125ml of the thick coconut milk. Place on a high heat and bring to the boil, then simmer for 1½ hours, partially covered. Stir occasionally to make sure the rice doesn't stick to the bottom of the pan.

Add both the sugars and salt and stir well. Continue to simmer for 30–40 minutes uncovered, adding extra water if the consistency of the pudding gets too thick. Discard the pandan leaves.

Serve the pudding in small bowls, with the remaining thick coconut milk and a drizzle of palm sugar syrup.

Banana Fritters with Miso Caramel

My dad would go so nuts for these fritters that I would need to take them away from him. My new addition is the miso caramel sauce, where the white miso brings an umami flavour kick to the banana fritters.

SERVES 6

125g self-raising flour
150ml sparkling water, cold
30g salted butter, melted and
    slightly cooled
35g caster sugar
1 teaspoon ground cinnamon
1 teaspoon Chinese five-spice
    powder
a pinch of salt
oil for deep-frying
4 ripe but firm bananas
icing sugar, to dust
toasted white sesame seeds,
    to garnish

For the miso caramel
200g soft brown sugar
200g unsalted butter, cubed
50ml double cream
3 tablespoons white miso paste

To make the banana fritter batter, mix the flour with half of the cold sparkling water to create a smooth paste. Stir in the melted butter. Whisk in the sugar, cinnamon, Chinese five-spice and salt until well incorporated, then gradually add the other half of the sparkling water.

Heat the oil in a clean wok/deep fryer to 180°C.

Meanwhile, make the miso caramel. Heat the sugar with the butter in a small saucepan until it's all melted, then stir well to mix together. Once it is bubbling away, whisk in the cream and miso. Remove from the heat.

Peel the bananas and cut each in half lengthways before cutting each half into 3 pieces horizontally.

Working in small batches, dip the banana pieces into the batter, then carefully lower into the hot oil and fry until golden brown. Remove and drain on kitchen paper.

Dust the banana fritters with icing sugar. Drizzle the caramel over the top and sprinkle with the toasted sesame seeds, or use the caramel as a dipping sauce.

This pandan mousse with meringue, English strawberries and mint is an exotic variation of the traditional Eton Mess. Taste the strawberries beforehand – if they are a little tart or need more flavour, cut them, sprinkle over some caster sugar and macerate for 15–30 minutes. Pandan essence may be hard to find but you can make your own by blending fresh pandan leaves with a touch of coconut milk or water (see Chendol Pudding on page 257). If you're tight for time, use shop-bought meringues.

Soften the gelatine sheets in a bowl of ice-cold water.

Meanwhile, whisk the egg yolks with the sugar in a large bowl or electric mixer until creamy. Mix together the coconut milk and pandan essence in a small saucepan and heat until simmering. Gradually whisk the coconut milk mixture into the egg yolk and sugar mixture, then pour back into the pan and gently heat the mixture to 83°C, stirring constantly. You're aiming for a custard texture so keep the heat low and the mixture moving constantly.

Transfer the custard to a bowl. Drain the gelatine sheets and squeeze out excess water, then whisk into the custard. Set the bowl over an ice-bath to cool, stirring occasionally, until the custard reaches 35°C or is cool to the touch. Whip the cream to soft peaks and fold through the chilled custard. Transfer to a serving bowl and chill for at least 6 hours.

If making the meringue, preheat the oven to 140°C/120°C Fan/ Gas Mark 1. Whisk the egg whites in an electric mixer until foamy. Combine the sugars and pass through a fine sieve to remove any lumps, then gradually add to the egg whites while whisking. Keep whisking until the meringue is glossy and will form firm peaks.

Spread the meringue on a baking tray lined with a silicone baking mat or baking parchment (not greaseproof paper or foil as meringue can stick to this), to a thickness of around 4–5mm. Bake for 1½ hours, then turn the oven off and leave the meringue in the oven overnight, to continue cooking in the heat of the oven as it cools.

To serve, scoop a portion of mousse into each bowl. Place strawberries on top, then roughly broken meringue and a scattering of fresh mint.

SERVES 6

For the mousse
6g gelatine sheets
2 medium egg yolks
50g caster sugar
125ml canned coconut milk
1 teaspoon pandan essence
200ml double cream

For the meringue
190g egg whites
190g caster sugar
150g icing sugar

To finish
a punnet of best-quality English strawberries, stems removed and quartered
a bunch of mint, leaves picked and finely sliced

Whenever I say I make my own Kaya, people are surprised, because they know how laborious it is to make. The process is like making a curd – you slowly cook the egg mixture over simmering water in a bain marie or double boiler. This means there isn't direct contact with the heat from the flames but instead a more gentle heat from the steam/water. Eventually, after a LOT of stirring, this results in a thick coconutty jam, which is perfect for toast and eggs. Be sure to use coconut cream, not the thinner milk, otherwise it takes much longer to cook. If you cannot find fresh pandan leaves, add a few drops of pandan essence at the beginning to give the pandan flavour as well as that bright green colour that my son loves. Refrigerated, Kaya will keep for 5 days, or less if you go through as much Kaya as my family.

Bring a large saucepan of water to the boil (the pan will need to hold a large heatproof bowl securely on top, with the base of the bowl just touching the water), then turn down to a simmer.

Crack all the eggs into the chosen large heatproof bowl and beat them together slightly. Add the sugar and whisk well to combine. Add the coconut cream and whisk until all incorporated, then add the knotted pandan leaves.

Place the bowl over the pan of simmering water. Using a spatula, slowly stir the egg mixture until it reaches a temperature of 83°C (no higher than this otherwise the egg will scramble), or until it coats the back of the spatula. This can take up to an hour of stirring. If you prefer the kaya to be thicker, more like a spread than a sauce, whisk in the cornflour slurry and cook for an extra 5 minutes, being careful not to go over 83°C.

Carefully lift the bowl off the pan of water and pour the kaya into a clean bowl, discarding the knotted pandan leaves. Place over a larger bowl of ice water to cool. Once cold, pour into sealed jars to store.

To serve, spread a thick layer of kaya onto a slice of toasted bread, add a heart-breaking amount of sliced butter and cut in half.

MAKES ABOUT 2 LITRES

10 large eggs
750g caster sugar
400g coconut cream (the really thick layer skimmed from the top of canned coconut milk)
4–5 pandan leaves, tied into a knot
1 teaspoon cornflour, mixed with a little water to a slurry (optional)

Ice Cream and Variations

I use this base for a lot of ice creams. It's so versatile and perfect for mixing with other flavours.

MAKES 1 LITRE

For the ice cream base
125g unrefined sugar
6 large egg yolks (120g)
500ml whole milk
1 teaspoon sea salt
100ml double cream

In a large bowl, whisk the sugar and egg yolks together. Heat the milk with the salt in a saucepan, stirring constantly, until it just comes to the boil. Slowly pour the hot milk mixture into the egg mixture, whisking constantly until fully incorporated.

Pour the mixture back into a clean saucepan and place on a low heat. Stir constantly using a spatula until the consistency of the custard is thick enough to coat the back of the spatula or reaches a temperature of 83°C maximum.

Pour the custard into a clean bowl and set over ice to stop the cooking process, stirring occasionally until cool. Whisk in the double cream. Strain through a sieve to remove any lumps of egg.

Put into an ice-cream machine and churn according to the manufacturer's instructions.

Variations

Coconut ice cream
Replace the whole milk with thick canned coconut milk (shake the can to mix the contents).

Vanilla ice cream
Scrape the seeds from 2 vanilla pods into the saucepan with the milk and salt. Add the pods to the pan too but don't forget to remove them before churning.

Kaya toast ice cream
Toast 4 slices of white bread and cut into 1cm cubes. Melt 100g butter in a frying pan and fry the bread cubes until golden. Drain on kitchen paper. Churn the ice cream base (preferably the coconut ice cream base). Just before the ice cream has finished churning, drizzle in Kaya (see page 249) to taste and add the buttered bread cubes.

Milo ice cream
Add 100g Milo powder into the hot custard and whisk in. For a richer finish, add more Milo – a large heaped tablespoon – while the ice cream is churning. My son loves a Milo Dinosaur sundae (see page 232): Milo ice cream finished with another heap of Milo on top with a touch of whipped cream. The smiles are worth it!

Soya Pudding with Palm Sugar

After I bought my Vitamix to help me make soy milk, I wanted to develop a recipe for soya pudding. It's one of those puddings that I would always seek out whenever I was in Chinatown buying ingredients. I would get an extra one for my mum, and we would sit on the sofa grinning at each other as we ate this fresh pudding that reminded us so much of Singapore. This recipe is served with palm sugar syrup for that coffee-like toasted flavour, but you could also serve it with ginger syrup (see the recipe for Sweet Potatoes in Ginger Syrup on page 239), or just a sugar syrup (page 266) for a less intense sweet flavour. Ideally use home-made soy milk instead of store-bought soy milk as home-made tends to be richer. If you use store-bought soy milk, you'll have to boil it longer to reduce it so it becomes rich and thick.

You need a coagulant to make the pudding – you can't substitute gelatine or agar agar otherwise you'll end up with a jelly. The two most common coagulants are gypsum (calcium sulphate) and nigari (magnesium chloride). If you have a local home-brewing supply shop, ask if they sell gypsum. Food-grade gypsum can also be purchased online. Always make sure you buy from a certified or trustworthy source.

Mix together the gypsum, cornflour and water in a bowl, stirring well to combine.

Bring the soy milk to the boil. As soon as it boils, skim off the foam/bubbles from the surface. Remove from the heat.

Stir the gypsum mixture again, then put it into a wide pot. Holding the pan of hot soy milk about 30cm above the pot, pour the milk slowly into the pot. This will make sure that the gypsum mixture is distributed evenly in the soy milk. *Do not stir.*

Cover the pot with a kitchen towel, being careful not to touch the surface of the milk, and then with the lid. Leave to set for about 1 hour, then scrape off the bubbly top of the pudding and discard it. To serve, use a shallow ladle to scrape the pudding into a serving bowl and add some syrup.

Tips:
To minimise the bubbles that form on the surface of the tofu pudding, skim off the foam/bubbles on the top of the soy milk and pour the soy milk gently into the diluted coagulant.

Make sure you stir the gypsum mixture well before pouring the soy milk into it. *Do not* do it the other way round, meaning pouring the gypsum mixture into the hot boiling soy milk.

SERVES 4

2 teaspoons gypsum
2 teaspoons cornflour or
  potato starch
85ml water
1.5 litres Home-made Soy Milk
  (see page 231)
Palm Sugar Syrup (see page 266)

Mango Pudding

I actually don't make this pudding that often because I struggle to find ripe mangoes that I think have enough flavour. It's the usual battle to find ingredients that are more like the ones in Southeast Asia. When I do get hold of good-quality mangoes, I always make this for my family. It's very cooling after a spicy meal. You can set this in small cups or bowls if you don't have ramekins.

SERVES 4

10g gelatine sheets or 7.5g
   powdered gelatine
160ml canned coconut milk
125g caster sugar, or more
   if needed
3 medium-sized mature mangoes
   (to yield 500g mango cubes plus
   extra to garnish)
60ml heavy cream, chilled
picked mint leaves, to garnish

Soften the gelatine sheets in a bowl of cold water.

Heat half of the coconut milk with the sugar in a small pan over a low heat. Drain the gelatine and squeeze out excess water, then add to the pan, or if using powdered gelatine, whisk well into the coconut milk. Keep stirring until the sugar and gelatine dissolve completely. Remove from the heat and set aside to cool.

Put 500g of the mango cubes in a blender with the remaining coconut milk and blend until very smooth. Mix the mango purée with the gelatine mixture and the cream, stirring until evenly combined, then strain the mixture (you may need to use a spatula to help push the mixture through the sieve).

Pour the mango mixture into ramekins and chill for 2–3 hours or until set. Before eating, decorate with the remaining mango cubes and mint leaves. Enjoy!

This is an old recipe that is being forgotten because there are now so many 'instant' mixes available, as well as chefs creating wildly modern versions. I don't mind that, but for me this is a true Chendol. Traditionally it is served with red kidney beans, but if you prefer it with salty coconut milk and palm sugar, like my son, that's fine. In the summer I fill the bowls with finely crushed ice (smash with a rolling pin in a sandwich bag under a tea cloth), then assemble the Chendol as instructed. It's such a lovely cooling pudding.

Blitz the pandan leaves in a high speed blender with 100ml of the water until it's all smooth and watery. Strain the liquid through a fine sieve lined with a wet J-cloth into a bowl; discard the pulp in the sieve. Pour the liquid into a saucepan and add the remaining water (or put all the water in the pan with the pandan essence). Whisk in the mung bean flour until it has all dissolved.

Whisk in the sugar and a pinch of salt. Place the pan on a medium heat, switch to a spatula and stir until the mixture has a paste-like texture with soft peaks, but be careful not to let it boil. It should drop slowly off the back of the spatula. Remove from the heat.

When just cool enough to handle, put the Chendol paste into a piping bag and cut off the end (a 2–3mm opening). Pipe the paste into an ice-bath or push through the holes of a slotted spoon or colander with the back of a ladle. I like to make 5–7.5cm lengths but it's up to your preference. Drain.

Mix the coconut milk with a pinch of salt. Serve the kidney beans, if using, with the piped Chendol paste in the bottom of small bowls. Pour over the seasoned coconut milk and palm sugar syrup.

SERVES 4

10 pandan leaves, sliced to about 2.5cm length (or use 1 teaspoon pandan essence)
650ml water
100g mung bean flour, sifted
45g caster sugar
500ml canned coconut milk
a 400g can red kidney beans, drained and rinsed well (optional)
100ml Palm Sugar Syrup (see page 266)
salt

pantry

These essentials are always lurking in my pantry, fridge or freezer because having them prepared means that dinner is a lot less stressful. I can whip up a meal in minutes with these at hand.

Some can be made ahead and stored. Sambal (chilli) sauces can be kept in sterilised jars, with a layer of oil on the surface, for up to a month. I make a big batch of curry powder rather than lots of little batches, and keep a large jar in the cupboard for when I want to make a chicken curry or spruce up a laksa base.

My mother's fridge is always full of these essentials: lots of jars of pickled chillies, of every kind, plus tiny little plastic bags of *rempahs*, dried shrimps and pastes. *Rempahs* freeze well so when you make one for a recipe, double the quantities and split off half to freeze for later use.

I highly recommend using the ice-cube tray trick for stocks (see pages 277–279). One of my favourite quick meals is based on frozen concentrated beef stock 'cubes' heated with some ho fun noodles, vegetables and leftover chicken. A great, healthy noodle dish that takes me 10 minutes to make.

Sambal Tumis Belachan

The best way to toast *belachan* is to break it up into a wok and dry-fry until really crumbly and toasted. This will produce a lot of aroma, so unless you want to have your home smelling of fermented fish, I'd recommend turning on the extractor fan to full blast and/or open as many windows as possible. This recipe makes a large amount, but the sambal keeps well in the fridge and I think it gets better over time. I use it on the side of a lot of my dishes.

MAKES 500G

8 candlenuts or macadamia nuts
2 lemongrass stalks
30 large, dried red chillies, soaked
   in warm water and drained
5 fresh, medium-hot, red Dutch
   chillies, roughly chopped
400g banana shallots, peeled and
   roughly chopped
5 garlic cloves, peeled
a 2.5cm cube of *belachan*
   (fermented shrimp paste),
   toasted (see above)
125ml cooking oil
3 tablespoons (about 45g)
   tamarind pulp, soaked in
   3 tablespoons hot water
60g palm sugar, grated

Grind the candlenuts, lemongrass, chillies, shallots, garlic and *belachan* together in a blender (adding the ingredients in the order listed) to make a paste (*rempah*), adding a splash of extra water if needed to help it blend together. Heat the oil in a wok or large saucepan on a medium-low heat and fry the *rempah* for 10 minutes, stirring frequently.

Meanwhile, press the tamarind mixture through a sieve to remove any seeds.

Add the sieved tamarind pulp to the *rempah* and continue to cook, stirring constantly, for at least 30 minutes up to 1 hour or until the oil separates. Add more oil if the mixture gets too dry.

Stir in the palm sugar until it melts completely and is fully incorporated. Set aside to cool, then store in an airtight container in a dry, cool place.

Chilli and Soy Sauce

Here is one of my mum's go-to condiments for every single dinnertime, without fail.

MAKES ABOUT
  1 TABLESPOON

1 fresh red chilli (bird's eye
   if you're feeling brave)
1 tablespoon soy sauce

Finely slice the chilli and add to the soy sauce, and serve in a small ramekin.

This sambal doesn't require hours stirring, but is just carefully blended together. It is perfect for cooking with, or mixing through vegetables.

Break up the *belachan* into cubes and toast in a frying pan or wok on a medium heat, using a wooden spoon or spatula to help break up the *belachan* and squash it against the side of the pan. Toast until fragrant, brittle and dry. Be careful not to burn.

Deseed the chillies if you prefer. Remove the stems and chop into rough small pieces. Grind the chillies with the kaffir lime leaf and toasted *belachan* in a blender (or using a mortar and pestle) until you have a fine dark paste. Season to taste with sugar and salt (remember that the *belachan* is naturally salty).

Store in an airtight container or jar in the fridge for up to a week. To use, put 2 tablespoons sambal into a small bowl and season with fresh lime juice (use more to tone down the pungent spice level).

MAKES ABOUT 90G

60g *belachan* (fermented shrimp paste)
3 fresh, medium-hot, red Dutch chillies
1 kaffir lime leaf (or Thai lime leaf), stem removed
caster sugar
salt if needed
2 small calamansi limes (or regular limes) to serve

Chilli and Lime Sauce

This chilli sauce is so bright, spicy and fresh; it's the perfect match for rice, noodle and meat or fish dishes. Add more or less sugar for sweetness, or lime juice for more acidity, and if you're making Hainanese Chicken Rice (see page 196), add a touch of the chicken broth and chilli sauce into a bowl to mix before serving.

Roughly chop the chillies, ginger and garlic, then grind together in a blender with the remaining ingredients until smooth. Add more or less sugar, vinegar and salt to your taste.

MAKES 250ML

80g fresh, medium-sized, red Dutch chillies
50g root ginger, peeled
6 garlic cloves, peeled
2 tablespoons toasted sesame oil
2 tablespoons fresh lime juice
35ml chicken stock (optional)
1 tablespoon caster sugar, or to taste
1 tablespoon rice vinegar, or to taste
salt

Crispy Chilli Oil

As a student I was addicted to Lao Gan Ma's Crispy Chilli in Oil, as it would go with everything from rice to noodle dishes or even scrambled eggs. I didn't realise what made it so addictive was the MSG added to it. If you don't want to use MSG, I recommend substituting with mushroom powder, like porcini for the unmistakable umami hit, or, like me, use both for the ultimate chilli crisp. Try to use kashmiri chillies to give the oil that bright gorgeous glow. Refrigerate in an airtight container in the fridge for up to 3 months.

MAKES AROUND 450ML

20g dried arbol chillies, stems and seeds removed

14g dried kashmiri chillies, stems and seeds removed

25g roasted salted peanuts, roughly chopped

a 2.5cm piece of root ginger, peeled and sliced into thin matchsticks

¼ teaspoon freshly ground black pepper

1 whole star anise

1 cardamom pod, spilt

1 teaspoon ground cumin

1½ tablespoons freshly ground Sichuan peppercorns

1½ tablespoons porcini powder (optional)

½ teaspoon MSG (optional)

1 teaspoon table salt

1 tablespoon caster sugar

250ml rapeseed oil, or any unflavoured oil

100g shallots, peeled and finely sliced

30g garlic, peeled and finely sliced

Use a spice grinder to blend the chillies in batches to grind them into flakes, and place them into a large heatproof bowl or pot. Add the peanuts, ginger, star anise, cardamom, cumin, ground Sichuan peppercorn, porcini powder and MSG (if using), salt and sugar. Set aside.

Place a fine mesh strainer over a bowl or saucepan. In another saucepan, heat the oil with the over a high heat, and the sliced shallots, constantly stirring until the shallots are golden brown. Strain the oil and shallots over the mesh strainer. Pour the oil back into the saucepan and heat again with the garlic and cook until golden brown. Pour the oil back over mesh strainer to separate the garlic from the oil. Set the shallots and garlic onto kitchen paper to remove the excess oil.

Return the oil back to the saucepan and heat again until it reaches 190°C. Once it reaches temperature, pour it over the spices and other seasonings. Stir well then set aside to cool down completely.

Once the chilli oil mixture has fully cooled down, remove the star anise and cardamom pods and mix in the golden garlic and shallots. Stir well and then pour into an airtight container or jars to store. It is to leave it for at least 24 hours to allow the flavours to develop.

Sambal Belachan (page 263) and
Chilli and Soy Sauce (page 262)

Palm Sugar Syrup

This is a very useful syrup to have on hand, especially for making desserts or adding to sambals (without the faff of having to grate or chop palm sugar). Palm sugar has rich coffee-like taste notes that really lift Singaporean and Malaysian dishes. Make sure you seek out real *gula melaka* (from the sugar palm sap) as there are fake palm sugars out there that tend to be on the sweet side.

MAKES 325ML

250g palm sugar, shaved or
   crumbled
125ml water

Gently heat up the sugar and water in a small saucepan until the sugar dissolves. Set aside to cool. The syrup can be kept in a jar or bottle in the fridge for 5 days.

Sugar Syrup

You can add flavours to sugar syrup to make perfect bases for drinks or puddings. Get creative with lemongrass ends, pandan leaves or even kaffir lime leaves.

MAKES 300ML

250g caster sugar
125ml water

Put the sugar and water in a saucepan and bring to the boil, stirring until the sugar has dissolved and the mixture is clear and has formed a syrup. Set aside to cool. The syrup can be kept in a bottle in the fridge for 5 days.

I use this curry powder in a lot of different recipes, as well as
sprinkling it over vegetables or for marinating meat, so I make it
in bulk to save time. It can be stored in an airtight container in
a cool dark place for around a month.

Warm up a large dry frying pan or wok, then toast the coriander
seeds for 4–5 minutes or until fragrant. Set aside. Next toast the
cumin and fennel seeds for about 2 minutes or until fragrant,
giving the pan a shake every now and then. Be very careful not
to let the spices scorch or burn.

Add the remaining spices and toast all together for about
5 minutes or until the mixture is warm and fragrant.

Transfer to a spice or coffee grinder, along with the coriander
seeds, and grind into a fine powder. You can do this in batches
if necessary. Tip on to a large tray and leave to cool, then store
in an airtight container in a cool dark place.

MAKES ABOUT 450G

225g coriander seeds
55g cumin seeds
30g fennel seeds
a piece of cassia bark
   (or a cinnamon stick)
3 cloves
20g white peppercorns
55g large dried red chillies
30g ground turmeric
½ nutmeg, grated
2 green cardamom pods

Nonya Fish Curry Powder

Very similar to the curry powder but this recipe just requires mixing
freshly ground spices together.

Mix all the spices together. Store in a jar in a cool, dark place for
up to a month.

**MAKES ABOUT
8 TABLESPOONS**

4 tablespoons ground coriander
1 tablespoon chilli powder
2 teaspoons ground cumin
2 teaspoons ground fennel
1 teaspoon ground white pepper
1 tablespoon ground turmeric
½ teaspoon ground cinnamon
a pinch of grated nutmeg
a pinch of ground cloves

Panch Phoron

Literally translating from Bengali as the Indian 'five spice blend' of equal amounts of seeds, this is used with our fish curry recipes but can also be used in cooking lentils, vegetables and meat dishes.

MAKES 5 TABLESPOONS

1 tablespoon cumin seeds
1 tablespoon nigella seeds
1 tablespoon fennel seeds
1 tablespoon mustard seeds
1 tablespoon fenugreek seeds

Mix all the spices together. Store in a jar in a cool, dark place for up to a month.

Shallot Oil and Crispy Shallots

Shallot oil and the garlic variation below are perfect finishing touches for noodles, noodle soups and congee. I always have them in my pantry. You can use the shallots for recipes that call for crispy shallots, and use the garlic in the same way.

MAKES 250ML

250ml vegetable oil
5 banana shallots, sliced thinly
salt

Heat up the oil to 160°C. Add the shallots and fry until golden. Remove the shallots with a slotted spoon and set aside to drain on kitchen paper. Add a touch of salt to the shallots.

Let the oil cool down completely before storing in an airtight container. Keep this in a cool, dry space. Store the shallots in an airtight container for up to 5 days.

Variation: Garlic oil

Thinly slice the cloves from 1 garlic bulb. Fry in batches in the hot oil until golden. As the garlic is fried, remove with a slotted spoon to kitchen paper to drain. Add a touch of salt while the garlic is still warm. Cool the oil completely and store in an airtight container in the fridge.

Sticky Teriyaki Sauce

I always have this super simple sauce in a squeezy bottle in the
fridge at home, for when I want to make a fast but tasty dinner.

Bring all the ingredients to the boil in a saucepan over a medium
heat. Boil until the sugar has dissolved. Use immediately or set
aside to cool, then bottle and keep in the fridge for at least
1 month.

MAKES ABOUT 450ML

150ml rice wine (shaoxing or sake)
150ml mirin
150ml dark soy sauce
3 tablespoons caster sugar

Tamarind Juice

We use tamarind a lot in our cooking to get those sweet
and sour notes. You can buy tamarind juice, or concentrate, but
there's nothing like squeezing and pressing your own juice from
the seeds for maximum freshness.

Add the tamarind pulp to the boiled water and leave to steep
for 10 minutes. Strain the juice into a bowl, using the back of a
spoon or ladle to press the juice through the sieve. Don't forget
to scrape the underside of the sieve to remove any sieved paste
there and add it to the bowl. The tamarind juice will keep in the
fridge for 5 days.

MAKES ABOUT 500ML

3 tablespoons (45g) tamarind pulp
500ml freshly boiled water

Variation
For 625ml juice use 100g tamarind pulp and 625ml water.

Smacked Cucumber (page 272)
and Nonya Mixed Vegetable
Pickle – Version 2 (page 275)

Pickled Green Chilli (page 273)
and Spicy Cucumber and
Pineapple Relish (page 273)

Smacked Cucumber

To make this even more special, add 1 tablespoon finely chopped garlic and smoked oil to the sauce. I advise you to try it!

SERVES 4 AS A SIDE

1 cucumber, about 300g
½ teaspoon salt
180ml Chinese red vinegar
120ml light soy sauce
3 tablespoons caster sugar
2 tablespoons chilli oil
1 tablespoon toasted sesame oil
1 teaspoon dried chilli flakes
   (or Korean red pepper flakes)
1 tablespoon toasted white
   sesame seeds

Cut the cucumber lengthways in half and remove the seeds with a teaspoon. Smack the cucumber with the back of a knife or a rolling pin, to slightly break it up. Slice the cucumber at an angle into 1cm pieces. Place in a bowl with the salt, mix well and set aside for 10 minutes.

Combine the remaining ingredients in a small bowl to make the sauce.

Rinse and drain the cucumber to remove the salt. Pour over the sauce and stir well, then serve. (If necessary you can keep this in the fridge for a day, but any longer and the cucumber will start to pickle too much.)

Pickled Green Chilli

This is the perfect addition to any fried noodle dish, so ideal to have
a handy supply in the cupboard.

Place the sliced chillies in a mixing bowl, add the salt and mix
well. Set aside. This salting will draw out the excess moisture from
the chillies while the pickling mixture is being prepared.

Put the vinegar and sugar into a saucepan and heat just to
dissolve the sugar. Leave to cool completely for 1–2 hours.

Rinse and drain the chillies and put them into a clean, sterilised
Kilner jar, discarding any extra liquid left behind from the salting.
Add the pickling mixture to cover the chillies. Leave to pickle for
a minimum of 24 hours before using. Store in a cool, dark place
for up to a month. Once opened, store in the fridge.

**MAKES ABOUT A 750ML
KILNER JAR**

200g large, fresh, mild green
    chillies, cut into 3mm slices
    (seeds in)
1 tablespoon salt

For the pickle
250ml rice vinegar
200g caster sugar

Spicy Cucumber and Pineapple Relish

This relish is great on the side of any dish, as it adds spice, acidity
and sweetness to a meal.

Combine the cucumbers and pineapple in a bowl. Add sambal
to taste. Season with the sugar and dark soy sauce. This is best
eaten the same day but can be kept in the fridge overnight.

SERVES ABOUT 4 AS A SIDE

2 cucumbers, peeled, deseeded and
    finely diced
½ pineapple, peeled, cored and
    finely diced
1 tablespoon Sambal Belachan
    (see page 263), or to taste
1 tablespoon caster sugar
½–1 tablespoon dark soy sauce

"Acar Awak"
Nonya Mixed Vegetable Pickle
– Version 1

There are two different ways to make Acar (pronounced 'ah-char'). The cooked version here involves blanching the vegetables first, which takes away some of the raw texture especially if using vegetables such as cauliflower. If you want a vegetarian pickle, omit the *belachan*.

SERVES ABOUT 6

1 cucumber
1 carrot, peeled
5–7 long beans, topped and tailed
2 litres water
75g cauliflower, cut into
    small florets
75g white cabbage, cored and
    chopped into bite-sized pieces
150ml cooking oil
250ml rice vinegar
4 tablespoons caster sugar
75g peanuts, roasted and
    roughly chopped
salt

For the rempah
a 3.5cm piece of fresh turmeric,
    peeled
7 banana shallots, peeled and
    roughly chopped
4 garlic cloves, peeled
2 fresh, medium-hot, red Dutch
    chillies, deseeded and sliced
7 large, dried, hot red chillies,
    soaked in warm water for 1 hour
    then drained
a 2.5cm (20g) piece of *belachan*
    (fermented shrimp paste),
    crumbled

Cut the cucumber in half lengthways and remove the seeds using a teaspoon. Cut the cucumber into 3.5cm long baton pieces. Do the same with the carrot and beans.

Heat up the water in a large saucepan with 1 tablespoon salt. Bring to the boil, then blanch the cauliflower for 1–2 minutes. Remove with a slotted spoon and set aside. Repeat the blanching process for the carrot, then the cabbage and green beans for 1 minute tops. Drain all the blanched vegetables and pat dry.

To make the *rempah*, grind all the ingredients together in a blender (adding them in the order listed) to form a fine paste. Heat the cooking oil in a large frying pan or wok on a medium heat. Add the *rempah* and stir-fry for about 5 minutes or until fragrant.

Add the blanched vegetables, rice vinegar, sugar and salt to taste. Stir well and bring to the boil for 2 minutes, then turn the heat down to a gentle simmer. Cook for 30 minutes, covered.

Cool completely, then stir in the peanuts. Store in an airtight container in the fridge for around a week.

Here is the cold pickle variation of the popular pickle recipe.

Cut the cucumber in half lengthways and remove the seeds using a teaspoon. Cut the cucumber into 3.5cm long baton pieces. Do the same with the carrot and beans and place in a big bowl with the cucumber. Cover with 50g salt and set aside for an hour.

Rinse the salted vegetables well with cold water, at least 3 times, to remove salt. Drain, spread out on a tray and pat dry.

To make the *rempah*, grind all the ingredients together in a blender (adding them in the order listed) to form a fine paste; add a splash of water to help blend if necessary.

Heat the oil in a large frying pan or wok on a medium heat. Add the *rempah* and stir-fry for about 10 minutes or until fragrant.

Add all the vegetables together with the rice vinegar, sugar and salt to taste. Stir well and bring to the boil for 2 minutes. Remove from the heat.

Add the peanuts, pineapple, if using, and sesame seeds. Cool and store in an airtight container in the fridge for up to a week.

SERVES ABOUT 6

1 cucumber
1 carrot, peeled
5–7 long beans, topped and tailed
150ml cooking oil
75g cauliflower, cut into small florets
75g white cabbage, cored and chopped into bite-sized pieces
250ml rice vinegar
4 tablespoons caster sugar
75g peanuts, roasted and roughly chopped
1 pineapple, peeled, cored and diced into small bite-sized pieces (optional)
1 tablespoon white sesame seeds, toasted
salt

For the rempah
4 candlenuts or macadamia nuts
2 lemongrass stalks (white parts), roughly chopped
10 banana shallots, peeled and roughly chopped
6 garlic cloves, peeled
12 fresh, medium-hot, red Dutch chillies, tops removed and roughly chopped
10 large, dried, hot red chillies, soaked in warm water for at least 1 hour and drained

Taré Sauce

The browned juices left at the bottom of a pan or baking tray when roasting meat have lovely flavour that is vital for sauces and gravies, so make sure you get every last bit from the pan. However, if the juices are black and burnt, do not use them as they will make your sauce taste bitter. Next time you roast meat, just remember to lower the temperature or reduce the length of the roasting time to prevent burning.

MAKES ABOUT 400ML

2–3 chicken backs and bones
  (ask your butcher)
225ml rice wine (shaoxing or sake)
225ml mirin
450ml light soy sauce
white pepper

Preheat the oven to 180°C/160°C Fan/Gas Mark 4. Break up the chicken bones into pieces and roast in a large non-stick baking tray for 30–45 minutes. You're aiming for perfectly browned bones and roasting juices caramelised at the bottom of the tray (fonds).

Transfer the roasted bones to a wide saucepan. Put the baking tray over heat on the hob and deglaze the fonds with some of the rice wine, using a spatula to scrape up the fonds and dissolve them in the hot wine. Add to the bones in the saucepan along with the remaining wine, the mirin and soy sauce. Bring to the boil, then simmer, uncovered, really gently for 1 hour.

Strain the sauce into a bowl, discarding the bones, and season well with white pepper. Set aside to cool before storing in an airtight container in the fridge for up to 5 days.

One thing I've learned in my time as a chef is that to obtain a great stock you should use a pressure cooker. It's the one piece of kitchen equipment I splurge on because I simply don't trust a cheap pressure cooker – they can be dangerous if not used or fitted correctly. With a pressure cooker you get a pure and intensely flavoured stock in half the time. I tend to make big batches of stocks, then reduce them and pour them into ice-cube trays, to use like I would a stock cube. If you don't have a pressure cooker, letting the stock simmer away on the stove will work just as well, although it will take double the time, but add a touch more water throughout cooking to keep everything covered in liquid.

Fish Stock

I use a mixture of fish and prawns for my fish stock – I find this really enhances the flavour of dishes that have a fish stock base such as laksa or soups. Fish stock doesn't take as long to cook as the meatier ones because you can obtain maximum flavour from fish bones quite quickly. Increase the amount of prawns if you want a stronger shellfish flavour. You could also add crab shells.

MAKES 1.5 LITRES

Place the fish bones in a large bowl in the sink and rinse under cold running water for about 5 minutes, or leave to soak in a bowl of water for 20 minutes. This helps remove any excess fish blood or impurities. Drain on kitchen paper and pat dry.

Peel the prawns and remove the heads. Set the shells and heads aside. Keep the prawns for other dishes – you can freeze them if they are fresh.

Heat the cooking oil in the bottom of the pressure cooker (or stock pot) and gently sweat the prawn heads and shells with the onions, carrot, spring onions, garlic and ginger for 20 minutes or until very aromatic and soft. Turn up the heat to high and cook for 4 minutes, then pour in the vermouth and wine, stirring well. Boil the liquid until it just about disappears. Add the fish bones, water and coriander stems. Put the lid on the pressure cooker and bring up to full pressure, then reduce the heat to low and cook for about 15 minutes. If doing this on the hob, simmer for 30 minutes, uncovered.

Remove the pressure cooker from the heat. Once safe to open, strain the liquid from the cooker through a sieve lined with muslin or a wet J-cloth into a large bowl. When cool, pour into ice-cube trays and freeze, or keep in the fridge for up to 5 days.

1.5kg white fish bones (ask your fishmonger for these)
1kg large raw prawns
2 tablespoons cooking oil
2 brown or white onions, sliced
1 large carrot, peeled and roughly chopped
5 spring onions, roughly chopped
3 garlic cloves, crushed
a 2.5cm piece of root ginger, peeled and thickly sliced
75ml dry vermouth
75ml Chinese cooking wine
1.5 litres water
a small bunch of coriander stems (optional)

Beef Stock

I always have this in my fridge or freezer. It's so useful for a quick beef noodle dish when my son is hungry. Just heat it up with some ho fun noodles and throw in some leftover cooked vegetables and you have a tasty 10-minute dinner!

MAKES 2 LITRES (OR ABOUT 650ML CONCENTRATED)

cooking oil

1kg beef bones (ask your butcher to chop these up into smaller pieces that will fit into your pressure cooker or pot)

400g oxtail, sectioned

2 litres water

5 onions, roughly chopped

5 carrots, peeled and roughly chopped

1 star anise

1 tablespoon black peppercorns

1 tablespoon coriander seeds, toasted

1 teaspoon cumin seeds, toasted

Preheat the oven to 200°C/180°C Fan/Gas Mark 6. Rub a little cooking oil over the bones and oxtail, then place these in a roasting tray in one layer. Roast for 35–40 minutes or until golden (you might need to turn the bones over once to help colour evenly).

Once nicely browned, use tongs to transfer the bones and oxtail to a large stock pot. Set the roasting tray aside. Cover the bones with cold water and bring to the boil. Pour a little of the boiling water into the roasting tray, scraping up the browned roasting juices from the bottom of the tray. Set this deglazing liquid aside.

Skim off any scum that comes to the surface of the boiling water, then drain the bones and rinse with cold water to remove any further impurities. Place the bones in the pressure cooker (or back into the stock pot) with the measured 2 litres of cold water and the deglazing liquid.

Heat 2 tablespoons cooking oil in a large saucepan on a medium heat. Fry the onions and carrots with the spices until well coloured and caramelised. Add to the pressure cooker.

Assemble the pressure cooker according to the manufacturer's instructions. Place on a high heat to bring to full pressure, then reduce and cook for 2 hours. If cooking on the hob, simmer gently for 4–5 hours.

Remove the cooker from the heat and, when it is safe to open, strain the stock through a sieve lined with muslin or a wet J-cloth into a large bowl. Set over an ice-bath to help the stock cool quickly, then place in the fridge to chill overnight or until the fat solidifies at the top. The next day, scrape off the fat and discard. If not reducing you can keep this stock in the fridge for up to 5 days.

If you want concentrated stock for freezing, after straining it boil it in a large pan until about a third of the liquid remains. Cool quickly, chill and remove the fat, as above. Heat the stock gently, then pour into ice-cube trays. Cool completely, then freeze. The stock 'cubes' will keep for a month.

Perfect as the base for noodle soups or in congee dishes.

Place the wings and/or carcasses in a large stock pot and cover with cold water. Bring to the boil. Skim off any scum that rises to the top, then drain and rinse the bones with fresh water. This will help to remove any impurities.

Place the wings/bones in a pressure cooker and add the measured water. Assemble the pressure cooker according to the manufacturer's instructions, put on the lid and bring to full pressure over a high heat. Reduce the heat and cook for about 1 hour.

Remove the pressure cooker from the heat and set aside to cool until the pressure has decreased completely. Once you can open the pressure cooker, add the remaining ingredients. Cover and place back on a high heat to bring to full pressure again. Reduce to a low heat and cook for about 1 hour.

Remove the cooker from the heat and, when it is safe to open, strain the stock through a sieve lined with muslin or a wet J-cloth into a large bowl. Set over an ice-bath to help the stock cool quickly, then place in the fridge to chill overnight or until the fat solidifies at the top. The next day, scrape off the fat and discard. This stock can be kept in the fridge for up to 5 days.

If you want concentrated stock for freezing, after straining it boil it in a large pan until about a third of the liquid remains. Cool quickly, chill and remove the fat, as above. Heat the stock gently, then pour into ice-cube trays. Cool completely, then freeze. The stock 'cubes' will keep for a month.

MAKES 2 LITRES (OR ABOUT 650ML CONCENTRATED)

2kg chicken wings / carcasses
2 litres water
4 pandan leaves, tied into a knot
6 spring onions (green part)
a 2.5cm piece of root ginger, peeled and thickly sliced
8 garlic cloves, peeled
5g black peppercorns
a bunch of coriander stems (optional)
1 tablespoon salt, or to taste

The main reason a lot of people don't have rice at home is because they don't know how to cook it. Lesson number one from my mum to me was: buy a good rice cooker! You don't need a fancy brand, but the best place to buy is Chinatown or an oriental store. Most rice cookers these days have clear markers on the inside to show the rice to water ratio, to make perfect fluffy rice. Failing that, my mum's trick is to put a (clean!) finger into the container of rice and water, and just touch the top of the rice. The water level should come up to the first segment of your finger (just under 2.5cm, if you have small fingers like me). Here is the saucepan method and the rice cooker method plus a couple of variations.

Saucepan method

Put the rice into a large bowl and cover with cold water. Swirl the rice around, then drain. Replace the water and repeat. Do this 3 times in all or until the water is clear. Give the rice a final rinse. Tip the rice into a saucepan and add the measured water. Bring to the boil over a high heat. Give the rice a good stir to prevent it from sticking immediately to the bottom of the pan, then boil the rice for a couple of minutes. When the rice starts to 'dance', turn the heat down to a gentle simmer. When the surface of the rice is almost dry, turn the heat right down to a minimum and cover with a tight-fitting lid. Cook for a further 10 minutes. Give the rice a fluff up before serving.

Rice cooker method

Rinse the rice as before (but not in the rice cooker bowl, as the rice will damage the non-stick coating). Put the rice into the rice cooker, cover with water (use the markers or my mum's finger test) and cook.

Variations:
Pandan steamed rice

I always add pandan to my rice because I love the aromatic flavour it gives. You can use Thai jasmine rice, broken rice or long-grain rice. Add 2 knotted pandan leaves to the rice before you cook it. Remove when serving.

Coconut rice

Replace 100ml of the 1.1 litres water with canned coconut milk. When fluffing up the rice, I like to fold in the thick coconut cream skimmed off the coconut milk, for extra richness.

SERVES 4–6

600g Thai jasmine rice (or broken or long-grain rice)
1.1 litres water

glossary

agar agar strips / powder

This is extracted from a variety of seaweed through an intense process of washing, sun-drying and boiling until it dissolves into a glutinous substance that is then dried and cut into strips or blended into a powder. Agar works in much the same way as gelatine does, but the texture of the set dish is slightly more firm – perfect for Nonya desserts – and it has a higher melting point than gelatine, which means an agar dessert will hold its shape if it gets warm.

anchovies, dried salted (*ikan bilis*)

These tiny little fish are served alongside dishes such as Nasi Lemak (see page 193). In the UK you can buy them in packets, either gutted or boiled. I use both. In Singapore they are sold from open sacks at dry goods stores.

banana leaves

Banana leaves are a common sight in Asian snacks (*kueh*) and desserts, as well as acting as wrappers for Otak Otak (see page 43) and sometimes Nasi Lemak (page 193). The supple leaves are non-stick and have a lovely sweet banana aroma. Give the leaves a good soaking before use. Scissors will cut the hard stem more easily than a sharp knife.

beansprouts

I buy these fresh only when they are shiny, white and perky, and not in bulk because they do not keep well. Never buy slimy, grey-looking beansprouts or those discoloured brown. You should remove the tops and tails – if you're lucky, this will already have been done for you. In the oriental store I used to go to in Islington, the Auntie would be sitting there plucking the tips off for her customers. I was always so grateful for this! Never eat beansprouts raw unless stated on the packet that they are 'ready to eat', and make sure when you blanch them that the water is at a rolling boil.

belachan

This is made from tiny shrimps that have been salted and fermented after which the paste is ground even smoother, then sun-dried, shaped into blocks and allowed to ferment again. I remember visiting a fishing village in Malaysia where they made *belachan*. You could smell the village long before it came into sight. But don't let the description 'fermented shrimp paste' or the smell put you off, because the natural umami, or savoury taste, of *belachan* is essential in this cuisine. *Belachan* is commonly found shaped into a block, wrapped in paper. The taste is very fishy and salty, and adding too much to a dish will overpower the other flavours. When pounding or blending it into a *rempah*, it's best to crumble it as much as possible first or chop it into smaller cubes. To release more 'aroma', I sometimes toast it in a dry wok. I did this once in the kitchen of our previous flat without opening any windows, and unfortunately the pungent smell lingered in our furniture for weeks. My husband banned me from doing this, so I had to get inventive and wrap up the crumbled *belachan* in foil to toast over the barbecue. You can toast the *belachan* dry, then use a spice grinder to make a powder, which is perfect for seasoning or adding to *rempahs*.

black fungus mushroom

Also known as wood-ear mushroom because of its ear-like shape, this fungus is normally dried, so needs to be soaked in hot water to rehydrate before use. We love this ingredient in soup dishes, because while it is pretty much tasteless, it provides a lovely chewy but crunchy texture.

black glutinous rice (*pulot hitam*)

Actually purplish in colour rather than black, this rice must be soaked overnight before using. Use it to make the dessert Bubur Pulot Hitam (see page 240).

black moss

Known as *fa cai*, which means prosperity (as in the good wish 'Gong hei fa cai' at Chinese New Year), this hair-like vegetable is actually dark green. It is added to dishes such as Chap Chai (see page 48), and thought to have a cleansing effect for the body.

cabbage

White cabbage is often used in Singaporean dishes because it's affordable and economical, being so large. I discard the outer leaves and cut out the hard core, then chop it to add to dishes such as Sayur Lodeh (see page 34) near the end of cooking, otherwise the cabbage will be overcooked and taste bitter.

calamansi lime (*limau kesturi*)

These limes are almost impossible to find in the UK (and very expensive if you do find one) but readily available in Singapore and Asia. Around the size of a large marble and with orange flesh, the sourness of the calamansi offsets a fishy flavour and chilli heat well. You can substitute an ordinary lime, but you might want to up the sweetness with sugar.

candlenut
(buah keras)

These nuts are toxic raw so if you are using them in the *rempah* for a dish, make sure that you cook out the *rempah* well. You can substitute macadamia nuts or cashews to obtain the same creaminess although these nuts won't help thicken sauces and dishes as candlenuts do.

cassia bark

Cassia bark is often misidentified as cinnamon bark. They are similar but cinnamon sticks are more commonly used in Indian cuisine, and the stronger cassia bark lends its fragrance to Chinese dishes.

chillies, dried fresh

I was always curious why my mum would buy 2 different types of chillies when we went to the shops. One bag would contain Dutch chillies – long, red and fleshy, and mild or medium-hot in heat. This type was developed in Holland so that the Dutch could replicate their favourite Indonesian dishes back in their homeland, far away from their previous colonies. My mum's other bag held the smaller bird's eye chillies, which are called *chilli padis*. These are insanely hot. She always complained the food here wasn't spicy enough so she would buy the Dutch chillies to cook with for us, but then use the hot chillies for herself. If I want to use chilli in a dish, but not add much heat, I slice the chilli in half and discard the white membrane and seeds inside as this is where the heat is found. When we were little, or growing up, if we were naughty, my mother would threaten to rub chilli on our gums or put it on our toothbrush. We always behaved after that threat because we totally believed her.

chillies, dried red

These contribute heat as well as red colour to a dish, essential in dishes like laksa. Before use, soak the chillies in warm water for at least an hour to rehydrate, then remove the stems and cut the chillies into pieces. I wear vinyl gloves so I don't touch my face. The chillies might be dried but they still have the burn!

**chinese fish cakes
/ fish balls**

Also known as fish slices, the 'cakes' are formed from blended fish that is steamed and sliced, or shaped first into blocks, then steamed and fried. They are commonly sliced to add to noodle dishes or soups. You can also mix the sliced fish cakes with cabbage and beansprouts in a stir-fry for a quick meal. Fish balls are the same, but much smaller, a perfect addition to soup dishes for extra protein. I normally keep a stash in the freezer for fast meals.

chinese rock sugar

This refined, crystallised sugar is found in small cubes or irregular lumps. It's most commonly used for adding sweetness and shine to dishes like Pork Rib Soup (see page 163). You can find it in most Asian supermarkets or substitute granulated sugar.

chinese sausage
(*lap cheong*)

Lap means 'preserved' and *cheong* means 'sausage'. There are different types, such as the sweet sausage made with fatty pork and the *gon cheong*, which is a liver sausage made from pork fat and duck liver. I always use the sweet type in cooking because it fries so well, perfect for egg fried rice or a claypot chicken and rice dish. Chinese sausage normally comes in vacuum-packed bags. Just slice the sausage up, as thick or thin as you'd like.

coconut milk

It's laborious making your own coconut milk and it's hard to get hold of fresh coconuts here in the UK, so I use canned coconut milk. My favourite brands are Amoy, Hom D or Chaokoh because they have a high coconut extract content. Check the can before you buy – you don't want anything less than 80 per cent coconut extract. The contents of the can will naturally separate into a layer of coconut cream on the surface of a thinner coconut milk beneath. For a thick coconut milk, shake the can to mix the contents. Alternatively, don't shake the can before you open it and you can scoop out the cream layer to add to dishes after the thinner coconut milk. This will prevent the cream from curdling or splitting, which would produce more oil in the end result.

coriander leaves

This is one of my favourite herbs, but I know many people detest it. It can be grown in a warm sunny spot in summer. In winter, indoors, I find using a UV light and frequent watering helps keep my coriander plant growing well.

fermented black
beans (*douchi*)

These aren't the Mexican black bean but a type of fermented and salted black soya bean, used most commonly for making black bean sauce for savoury dishes like stir-fries of fish and meat or Ma-Po Tofu (see page 111).

fermented soya beans (*taucheo*) and paste (*taucu/ tauchu*)

This lends saltiness and depth of flavour to a dish, similar to miso but sweeter. *Taucheo* are whole beans. Some bottled versions of the paste contain whole beans while others are more mashed up. If there are beans present it's best to mash them before using so the paste blends evenly into the dish. The main commercial brand is Yeo's (Yeo Hiap Seng).

fermented soya-bean curd

Similar to fermented soya beans and paste, this curd (also called preserved tofu) adds a delicious saltiness and tang to a dish. You'll find small cubes of preserved curd in jars.

galangal (*lengkuas*)

Also known as blue ginger or wild ginger, this root/rhizome is very similar to ginger apart from the shiny appearance of its skin. Because it is so hard and fibrous it needs to be peeled and sliced across the fibres, then sliced again into matchsticks before pounding. Galangal can be frozen, but don't try to slice it before it thaws – this is near impossible.

ginger

Ginger is used in many Asian dishes. When young its skin can be peeled away easily using the edge of a spoon, otherwise use a peeler. Don't be tempted to cut off the skin as this will waste lots of ginger. Ginger tea is a great remedy when you're feeling queasy or unwell. Or for sore joints, rub a slice of ginger directly on to the skin – my mum used to do this for me.

gochujang paste (hot chilli paste)

We absolutely love Korean food in our household, and gochujang is a key ingredient. It is a fermented red chilli paste that has savoury and sweet flavours. Use for marinating meats, stir into dipping sauces or add to soups to punch up. Depending on the brand, the spiciness of the chilli paste can vary from hot to extremely hot so use with some caution.

kaffir lime leaves (*duan limau purut*)

These small fragrant leaves have a citrusy scent that I adore. They can be used whole in cooking, or if they are to be eaten, for dishes like laksa or Beef Rendang (see page 203), first remove the hard middle stem, then fold the leaf and slice thinly. In Singapore I would break a couple of leaves off my mum's plant, and rub them around my ankles to act as a mosquito repellant – they don't like the citrus smell or taste.

laksa leaves
(daun keson)

Super hard to find in the UK, these slim, pointed leaves are torn for their fragrance and zing that adds that extra something to laksa dishes or Asam Ikan Pedas (see page 44). The leaves are also known as Vietnamese hot mint.

lemongrass
(seray)

This is an essential ingredient in Nonya cuisine, lending a sharp, lemony tang to dishes. The thick, tough outer layer and the top third of the stalk should be discarded because they are dry. If you intend to pound or grind lemongrass, first chop it into very fine slices, otherwise you'll be grinding for hours as it is so fibrous. Sometimes I use a lemongrass stalk whole in a dish, crushing it first using the back of a knife to release its aroma, then remove before serving.

lily buds, dried

Before using, these edible flowers are soaked in hot water to soften them. I trim them down to make them easier to eat. Dried lily buds are said to have diuretic properties.

long beans

These beans live up to their name, being about 30cm long for best flavour and texture. Found in oriental supermarkets, they are perfect for Acar Awak (see page 274) or Sayur Lodeh (page 34).

palm sugar
(gula melaka)

Usually found in slightly moist, dark brown, firm cylinders, this is made from the sap of the coconut palm. It is scraped or grated before using in syrups to add to most Nonya desserts or treats. Palm sugar has a rich, smoky, toffee-like flavour that cannot be replaced by any other sweetener. Be warned that there are many fake *gula melakas*, which have a much higher content of white sugar.

pandan leaves

The essence derived from pandan leaves is the Asian counterpart to vanilla essence, although I think it's much more than that. It has almost an almond biscuit flavour when used with coconut in desserts, and also an incredible savoury note that works well with chicken, such as for Hainanese Chicken Rice (see page 196). Fresh leaves are mainly used in cooking, tied into a knot to release the aroma then thrown into a rice cooker or other pot. To extract a pandan liquid essence you can blitz the leaves in a blender with water, then pass through a very fine sieve lined with a wet J-cloth. You can buy pandan essence but it tends to contain additives and colouring.

pork floss
(*rousong*)

Also known as meat wool and meat floss, this has a light and fluffy texture. It is commonly used as a topping for congee, tofu, savoury soy milk and, one of my favourites, in soft buns. You can use chicken or fish to make meat floss, but pork is the most common. It's made exactly like pulled pork: the meat is blanched, then cooked with flavouring, pulled apart into shreds, and finally stir-fried until dry.

rice

The preferred type of rice in our household is Thai Hom Mali jasmine rice. Its fluffy white character makes a perfect base for Peranakan dishes. As when buying diamonds, don't settle for the cheapest. I can always tell when a crop of rice isn't the best because it has a different texture and flavour. For cooking rice, I recommend you use a rice cooker. It's so easy and takes a lot of the stress out of cooking a meal. I can't emphasise enough how important this one gadget is to me in our kitchen and you can get hold of a decent one for £20. I always add just enough water to cover the rice and come 1cm above it – to the first line on my pinky finger.

rice cakes,
compressed
(*lontong*)

If I have any leftover warm cooked rice, I usually make compressed rice cakes. The traditional way to make them is to stuff banana leaves with the rice and boil for around 4 hours. As I usually cannot find banana leaves easily here, instead I press the rice into a loaf tin or cake tin and cool, then turn out and slice into 2.5cm cubes. Use compressed rice cakes in dishes like Sayur Lodeh (see page 34) or as a side dish to accompany satays.

salted preserved
radish (*chai poh*)

This is white radish (mooli) or turnip that has been heavily salted and chopped up. It adds saltiness to dishes like Fried Carrot Cake (see page 184). My mum calls it 'vegetarian caviar' because of its distinctive crunch and umami flavour that 'pops' in the mouth. Some brands can be very salty, so I recommend tasting it first; if it's too salty, especially for children's taste, rinse it under cold water a couple of times and then dry well. It's perfect in omelettes or sprinkled over congee.

sesame paste

Not to be confused with tahini (which tends to be made with more oil, and sometimes flavoured oil), for Chinese sesame paste the seeds are first toasted (or roasted) and then ground to make a dark, really thick, almost hard paste. You'll normally find a layer of sesame oil on top. It's hard to find decent sesame paste, so I make my own by roasting sesame seeds and blending in batches with unflavoured oil and salt until smooth.

shallots

Shallots in Asia are a lot smaller than the ones found here in the UK. They are also more intense in flavour and heat. I tend to use one large banana shallot to represent 4 small Thai shallots in converting recipes and adjust the heat level to where I want it.

shiitake mushrooms, dried

Soak these in hot water for at least 20 minutes before using, then rinse and squeeze out any excess water before slicing. The stems tend to be tough and hard so discard them.

shio koji

This is a Japanese paste made by fermenting *koji* (grains such as rice or barley that have been inoculated with Aspergillus oryzae, the mould that gives us miso, soy sauce and sake) with water and salt (*shio*) and then blending until thick. It's super rich in enzymes so perfect for marinades and also blending into sauces to add more umami.

shrimps, dried (*udang kering*)

These are quite salty, so rinse with water to remove some of the saltiness, then soak in hot water for a few minutes to soften. Drain and pat dry before pounding or blending.

spring onions

The whites of spring onions are often sliced finely and used to garnish soups and other dishes. Make sure you rinse spring onions well as dirt can get stuck inside the layers. After chopping, I rinse them again with iced water to 'crisp' and refresh them. If you put the root ends in water, you can watch the onions begin to regrow.

tamarind (*assam*)

Tamarind pulp lends a sour plum-like tang to dishes. The trees from which the pods come are native to Africa but are prevalent in India where there is even a state called Assam. The preserved pulp is made up of several seeds, coated with a glutinous flesh. Before use it needs to be steeped in hot water for at least 10–20 minutes, then squeezed in damp muslin or pushed through a fine sieve with the back of a spoon or ladle. When doing this you want to extract as much as possible to form a concentrate.

tofu, firm (*taukua*)

To make firm tofu (bean curd), the curd is pressed to extract the liquid or whey. The longer it is pressed, the firmer it will be. You can make taukua by sandwiching the curd between towels or kitchen paper and setting a baking tray and then a weight (such as cans of food) on top. Firm tofu keeps its shape well during cooking. If you buy it packed in liquid, drain it on some kitchen paper before cooking to soak up as much excess liquid as possible.

tofu, silken

Silken tofu is unpressed and undrained, so is usually formed in a container. Compared to other types of tofu, it has the highest water content and lowest protein content. Drain it well before using, but handle carefully as its jelly-like consistency is delicate.

tofu, soft (*tauhu*)

With its soft creamy texture, *tauhu* is perfect for light soups such as the Watercress Soup on page 152. Before using, just drain off the excess water.

tofu puffs, deep-fried (*taupok*)

These are made by extracting the liquid from tofu (bean curd) and then deep-frying the tofu to produce a 'puff' that is soft and spongy on the inside and crispy on the outside. Tofu puffs are perfect for dishes like Chap Chai (see page 48) or to add to laksas, as the puffs soak up the flavoursome stock or sauce and, when you bite into them, they are deliciously juicy.

tofu sheets / skin

Also called soya-bean or bean-curd sheets / skin, these thin dry sheets are used for wrapping food, such as Ngo Hiang Rolls (see page 56). Wipe the sheets with a damp J-cloth before use to make them more pliable, otherwise they will snap and break as you roll them.

torch ginger flower (*bunga kantan*)

Bunga kantan is what gives the distinctive sour taste to many iconic Malaysian dishes, such as Asam Laksa, Asam Ikan Pedas (see page 44), Nasi Kerabu and more. Unlike the chilli, it's a local ingredient that is almost impossible to find in Western shops, so I use fresh citrus, tamarind and laksa leaf as substitutes. Torch ginger flowers are pink, red or white. The bud is the most commonly used part in cooking, but the whole plant is edible. In Sarawak the Kelabits cook the inner buds of the opened blossom like a vegetable in stir-fries.

turmeric (*kunyit*)

Turmeric lends a bright yellow colour to the dishes it is used in, as well as an earthy mustardy flavour. If using fresh turmeric rhizome/root, peel the skin and slice into fine matchsticks before grinding or pounding. Dried turmeric is really useful if you don't have access to fresh.

white miso paste (*shoyu*)

Miso means 'fermented beans' in Japanese, and in this case it refers to soya beans that are blended with a grain (like rice or barley), salt and koji (mould). The white or light miso (sometimes called sweet miso) tends to be sweeter and lighter in flavour thanks to a shorter fermentation time. It's made with less soya bean content and more grains like white rice. The paste adds an incredible umami flavour to dishes, but I always use carefully because despite white miso being the sweeter miso, it can still be salty in large quantities.

wonton skins / wrappers

Wontons are the most popular snacks in Chinese cuisine. There are different ways to cook them, from deep-frying or adding to soup to steaming and serving with chilli oil. They are fairly simple to make if you have a pasta machine; however, I find it easiest to buy a packet to keep for when they are needed. We fill them with lots of different mixtures from pork mince, water chestnut, or mushroom and chive, and serve with chicken broth for a delicious dinner.

stockists

Growing up, we lived in Maidenhead so my mother would have to improvise a lot of ingredients from what she could get at the local supermarket or Asian grocery store, so a lot of the recipes aren't what I'd call 'authentic', but when we required the specialist ingredients such as candlenuts, galangal or good quality lemongrass, we would travel to Chinatown or drive to Wing Yip, which tended to be on a monthly basis. Thankfully, these days most shops and produce are available online for delivery so here is my recommended list.

general Asian ingredients

Wing Yip
395 Edgware Road,
Cricklewood,
London, NW2 6LN
www.wingyip.com

See Woo
18–21 Lisle Street
London, WC2H 7BE
www.seewoo.com

Loon Fung
42–44 Gerrard Street
London, W1D 5QG
OR
1 Glacier Way,
Alperton,
Wembley HA0 1HQ
www.loonfung.com

Wai Yee Hong
Eastgate Oriental City
Eastgate Road
Bristol, BS5 6XX
www.waiyeehong.com

Longdan
25 Hackney Road
London, E2 7NX
www.longdan.co.uk

Tawana
15–20 Chepstow Road
London W2 5BD
www.tawana.co.uk

Japan Centre
35b Panton Street
London, SW1Y 4EA
www.japancentre.co.uk

online

Mei Mei – for sambals, sauces, essential produce
www.meimei.uk

Sous chef – for specialist ingredients and equipment
www.souschef.co.uk

ChefsLocker – for Japanese barbeques or knives
www.chefslocker.co.uk

Kitchen Provisions – for knives, specialist equipment and decorations
www.kitchenprovisions.co.uk

Natoora – for restaurant quality seasonal produce
www.natoora.co.uk

conversion tables

weights

Metric	Imperial
15g	½oz
20g	¾oz
30g	1oz
55g	2oz
85g	3oz
110g	4oz / ¼lb
140g	5oz
170g	6oz
200g	7oz
225g	8oz / ½lb
255g	9oz
285g	10oz
310g	11oz
340g	12oz / ¾lb
370g	13oz
400g	14oz
425g	15oz
450g	16oz / 1lb
1kg	2lb 4oz
1.5kg	3lb 5oz

liquids

Metric	Imperial
5ml	1 teaspoon
15ml	1 tablespoon or ½fl oz
30ml	2 tablespoons or 1fl oz
150ml	¼ pint or 5fl oz
290ml	½ pint or 10fl oz
425ml	¾ pint or 16fl oz
570ml	1 pint or 20fl oz
1 litre	1¾ pints
1.2 litres	2 pints

length

Metric	Imperial
5mm	¼ in
1cm	½in
2cm	¾in
2.5cm	1in
5cm	2in
10cm	4in
15cm	6in
20cm	8in
30cm	12in

useful conversions

1 tablespoon = 3 teaspoons
1 level tablespoon = approx. 15g or ½oz
1 heaped tablespoon = approx. 30g or 1oz
1 egg = 55ml / 55g / 1fl oz

oven temperatures

°C	°C Fan	Gas Mark	°F
110°C	90°C Fan	Gas Mark ¼	225°F
120°C	100°C Fan	Gas Mark ½	250°F
140°C	120°C Fan	Gas Mark 1	275°F
150°C	130°C Fan	Gas Mark 2	300°F
160°C	140°C Fan	Gas Mark 3	325°F
180°C	160°C Fan	Gas Mark 4	350°F
190°C	170°C Fan	Gas Mark 5	375°F
200°C	180°C Fan	Gas Mark 6	400°F
220°C	200°C Fan	Gas Mark 7	425°F
230°C	210°C Fan	Gas Mark 8	450°F
240°C	220°C Fan	Gas Mark 9	475°F

about the author

Although born in Singapore, Elizabeth Haigh has spent most of her life living in Berkshire, and now lives with her husband and son. On her annual visits back to Singapore to visit family and friends, she would soak up all the humidity, food, traditions and respect for different cultures.

Having studied Architecture at Central St Martins, she competed on BBC 1's *MasterChef*, before becoming a recognised chef in London. *Elle* magazine described her as 'the most exciting new superchef around' on their 2020 list, and she has been featured in the *Evening Standard*'s Progress 1000 and in *Vogue* magazine.

A passionate advocate for Singaporean cuisine, Elizabeth is the owner and founder of Mei Mei restaurant and *kopitiam*, in Central London that Jimi Famurewa described as 'a wholly addictive act of cultural celebration'.

@the_modernchef / *@meimeilondon*

acknowledgements

Since becoming a mother myself, to Riley, I realised that we had no reference to our family's recipes, other than asking my mother and I wanted to rectify that, if anything to honour our favourite hobby of cooking in print so I could pass this onto my children, and their children.

I've long felt that Singaporean and Malaysian cuisine in general needs more representation and understanding, and I'm so grateful that my agent, Martine Carter, and publishers, Absolute, saw the potential far before anyone else did.

However, this book wouldn't exist at all without my mother, for her wisdom, patience, and passion for cooking and providing for us all this time. She would go above and beyond, working long hard hours and coming home and whipping up a three or four dish dinner for the family. Despite not saying it enough, I'm so grateful for everything she's done for us as a family. Learning and understanding about our heritage and culture makes me feel richer than any money ever could.

As much as my mother would teach me flavour, my father, Trevor, taught me about the passion for eating. Without appreciating food, it's easy to think of food as more of a necessity than a pleasure. My father's table manners would immediately go out the window when he was presented with good food, because it was his joy to eat, and this is something I wish I understood more when I was younger and being bullied for liking food that was seemingly 'different'. Thank you both for opening our eyes to a world of cuisine that has inspired me to become a chef, and not putting up too much of a fight when I said I wanted to become a chef after years of training to become an architect.

Also thank you Dad, for spending hours transcribing and typing up our family recipes for me to work on. My sisters, Sarah and Jane, who have put up with me talking about this book for years now, and have always supported me in everything I've done. I hope I've done you all proud with this one.

Thank you to my husband Steele, who's always been my rock, my role model, best friend and a huge supporter of my work, who's done way more than his fair share of childcare for Riley whilst I panicked about deadlines, working on *Makan*, balancing my work and the business. We both knew that me taking on a book, looking after Riley and starting a restaurant would be a huge ask but I couldn't have done it without your love and support. I love you very much and may we continue this Kaizen journey together.

A thank you to my grandparents, my Por Por and Gong Gong, aunties and uncles and my extended family in Singapore. We live far apart but my mother and this book is our constant connection and reminder of our life there. I still dream about eating durian on the cold marble floor, over newspapers or playing mahjong, badly, with so much joy.

Of course, a huge thank you to my amazing publishers, Jon Croft, Meg Boas and Emily North at Absolute who seem to have patience like saints whilst I wrote this at the same time as opening a restaurant. It's been a dream to work with you all, especially during the hardest year for everyone. Just knowing you were after my book proposal for a long time meant that I knew the book would be in great hands. May we continue to have long lunches with wine in Bath again soon.

Thank you to my incredible photoshoot family: art director Peter Moffat for bringing my scribbles to this beautiful representation of *Makan*, to Kris Kirkham for shooting and styling *Makan* so perfectly. The fact that you also felt the same connection to this food made it less daunting that we were shooting so many recipes for my first book. I was more nervous shooting this book and getting it spot on than I was for cooking for Michelin inspectors. It was such a joy and ease to work with you: it makes me feel like all photoshoots should be that easy and enjoyable.

Thank you to Frankie Reddin and Anna Masing from A + F Creative, who put up with a lot of late-night emailing, meetings fuelled with wine and long discussions about diversity, representation and helping me to make all my many mad ideas into actual sense. As well as being rock stars and good friends, you're the best PR team any chef could ask for.

Thank you for my dream team at Mei Mei – Chef Christian, Clara, Rolaine, Ben, Chris, Julio and Chloe for being so patient with me whilst I wrote *Makan*. It felt like having two dreams come true in writing a cookbook and also opening a restaurant in the same year, but I never appreciated what a mammoth task that would be. However, it didn't feel quite so mammoth knowing the team would always have my back. Thank you for your support and understanding when I was tired and grumpy from writing all night then coming in at 8am to do the morning shifts. Your passion and energy as a team pushes me to be a boss that you'd be proud to work for.

This leads nicely to our friends and supporters of the Mei Mei and my work as a chef. Without you, I'd lack any sort of confidence that I was on the right track. Particularly a shout out to Chris and Turid, Kyle, Kyrenia and the twins, Hugh and Beth, for always coming to my pop-ups, the support and good humour.

Lastly, thank you readers. Not only are you supporting me, you are supporting diversity in writing and cooking. I hope this book brings you as much joy and love as it does me, and will be well used to be passed on to future generations.

Liz x

BLOOMSBURY ABSOLUTE
Bloomsbury Publishing Plc
50 Bedford Square, London, WC1B 3DP, UK
29 Earlsfort Terrace, Dublin 2, Ireland

BLOOMSBURY, BLOOMSBURY ABSOLUTE, the Diana logo and the
Absolute Press logo are trademarks of Bloomsbury Publishing Plc

First published in Great Britain 2021

A catalogue record for this book is available from the British Library.

Library of Congress Cataloguing-in-Publication data has been
applied for.

HB: 9781472976505
ePub: 9781472976499
ePDF: 9781472976512

2 4 6 8 10 9 7 5 3

Printed and bound in China by C&C Offset Printing Co. Ltd, China

Bloomsbury Publishing Plc makes every effort to ensure that the papers
used in the manufacture of our books are natural, recyclable products
made from wood grown in well-managed forests. Our manufacturing
processes conform to the environmental regulations of the country of
origin.

To find out more about our authors and books visit www.bloomsbury.com
and sign up for our newsletters.

Publisher
Jon Croft

Commissioning Editor
Meg Boas

Art Direction and Design
Peter Moffat

Junior Designer
Anika Schulze

Senior Project Editor
Emily North

Photographer
Kris Kirkham

Photographer's Assistant
Eyder Rosso

Food Styling
Elizabeth Haigh

Copyeditor
Norma MacMillan

Proofreader
Margaret Haynes

Home Economist
Elizabeth Fox

Indexer
Zoe Ross